the Inviting WORD

**A Worship-centered, Lectionary-based
Curriculum for Congregations**

Learner's Guide for Older Youth

Year 3

United Church Press

Cleveland, Ohio

Thomas E. Dipko	Executive Vice President, United Church Board for Homeland Ministries
Audrey Miller	General Secretary, Division of Education and Publication
Lynne M. Deming	Publisher
Sidney D. Fowler	Editor for Curriculum Resources
Kathleen C. Ackley	Associate Editor for Curriculum Resources
Monitta Lowe	Editorial Assistant
Marjorie Pon	Managing Editor
Kelley Baker	Editorial Assistant
Paul Tuttle	Marketing Director
Linda Peavy	Associate Marketing Director
Madrid Tramble	Production Manager
Martha A. Clark	Art Director
Angela M. Fasciana	Sales and Distribution Manager
Marie Tyson	Order Fulfillment/Inventory Control Manager

Writers

Charlene Zuill, writer of the lessons for Propers 17 and 18, is an associate pastor working with youth at Holman United Methodist Church in Los Angeles, California. She is interested in the empowerment of African American youth and issues of diversity.

Ted Huffman, writer of the lessons for Propers 19 and 20 and Pentecost Sunday through Proper 17, is senior minister of First Congregational UCC in Rapid City, South Dakota.

Pamela Dilmore Hadsall, writer of the lessons from Pentecost to Proper 16, is a writer and a United Methodist pastor currently serving Christ United Methodist Church in Springfield, Missouri. She writes a wide variety of materials for the United Methodist Publishing House.

Hamilton Coe Throckmorton, writer of the lessons for Lent 1 through Easter 3, is the senior pastor of Barrington Congregational Church in Barrington, Rhode Island. He is one of the writers for the *Affirming Faith* confirmation resource. Hamilton is married to Mary Senechal and has two sons, Alexander and Taylor.

Editor

Laurel Hayes, the editor for older youth, is an ordained minister in the United Church of Christ and the Executive Secretary of the Council for Ecumenical Student Christian Ministry (CESCM). She is also a doctoral candidate in religion and education at Union Theological Seminary and Teachers College, Columbia University.

United Church Press, Cleveland, Ohio 44115
© 1996 by United Church Press

Design

Kapp & Associates, Cleveland, Ohio

Cover art

Linda Post, *Solstice*, R. Michelson Galleries, Northampton, Mass. Used by permission of R. Michelson Galleries.

God makes it possible for people to take leaps of faith, trusting that they will land safely.

Linda Post, *Solstice*, R. Michelson Galleries, Northampton, Mass.
Used by permission of R. Michelson Galleries.

welcome

Welcome and Information Sheet

Welcome to *The Inviting Word!* During this year you and your friends can expect to encounter God springing forth from the Word in many different ways as you learn and grow with *The Inviting Word*. Some weeks you may want to sit silently with God's Word. Other weeks the Word may make you want to jump with joy. Whatever your response to the Word, you will be invited to offer it up in song, silence, and prayer. The Word will encourage you to take leaps of faith as you think and dream about your own life and the world around you. However, you will never be leaping into a void. God and God's people will be there to catch you and to support you. Plunge in!

Don't hide your light under a bushel! Please complete the form below and return it to your leader(s).

Name ....

Address ....

Telephone number ....

Birth date ....

Year in school ....

Parent(s) or guardian(s) ....

Address ....

Telephone number ....

Have you been baptized? If so, when and where? ....

....

If you were baptized as an infant, have you been confirmed? If so, when and

where? ....

What are your special interests or hobbies? ....

....

....

What talents would you be willing to share with this group? ....

....

....

What are your hopes for this group? ....

....

....

Contents

Moses, Moses!

Moses looked, and the bush was blazing, yet it was not consumed. Then Moses said, "I must turn aside and look at this great sight, and see why the bush is not burned up." When God saw that Moses had turned aside to see, God called to him out of the bush, "Moses, Moses!"

Exodus 3:2b–4a

Fire is the first and final mask of my God.

Nikos Kazantzakis, *The Saviors of God: Spiritual Exercises* (New York: Simon and Schuster, 1960), 128.

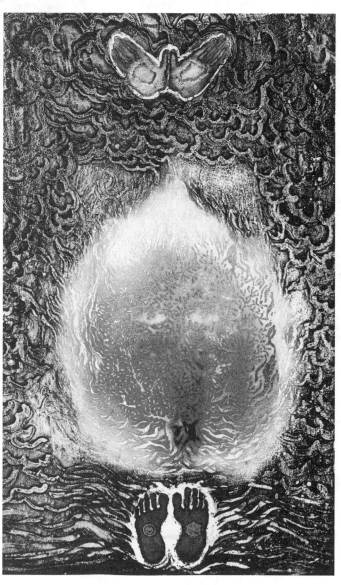

Paul Koli, *The Burning Bush*, as reproduced in *The Bible Through Asian Eyes*, ed. Masao Takenaka and Ron O'Grady (Auckland, New Zealand: Pace Publishing in association with the Asian Christian Art Association, 1991), 41. Used by permission of the Asian Christian Art Association.

A Real Heavy Message

Moses' gig was to care for the flock of sheep that belonged to his father-in-law. One day he went out to the desert with the flock next to a place called Horeb, the very mountain of the Almighty. And right there, in the midst of a burning bush, the Angel of the Almighty appeared to Moses. Even though there was a fire, the leaves and branches didn't even seem to burn.

"Goodness," said Moses. "What's happenin' here?"

The Almighty raised His voice and called, "Moses. Moses."

"I'm here," said Moses.

And the Almighty said, "Take your shoes off, son. This is holy ground."

(continued on side 2)

What does this painting stir in you?

God knows each one of us by name.

7

God is a sustainer, judge, deliverer, guide, worthy of worship.

(continued from side 1)

Moses scrambled 'round to do as he was told.

Then the Almighty said, "I am the Almighty of your father, the Almighty of Abraham, the Almighty of Isaac, and the Almighty of Jacob. I'm the one."

Moses was afraid, but the Almighty continued. "I've had my eye on the children of Israel who are in Egypt and I know how rough it's been for them. I'm gonna take them away from all that and bring them to a land flowing with milk and honey. And you, son, are gonna help me."

"You gotta be kidding," said Moses. "I ain't nobody to be doing something like that."

And the Almighty said, "I ain't sending you alone. I'll be there."

"All right, that sounds cool. So what? Even if you're with me and all, why should the children of Israel follow me? They'll ask questions. I ain't got the answers. What'll I say when they ask who sent me?"

The Almighty said to Moses. "Just tell 'em, 'I AM WHO I AM.' Tell 'em, I AM has sent you.

"Also, tell them that the Almighty of their fathers, Abraham, Isaac, and Jacob, has sent you. I ain't changed. I'm working this only 'cuz of my promise to their fathers. Don't worry. They'll listen to you. I promise."

And the Almighty got down to business with Moses, explaining to him what he should do.

P. K. McCary, interpreter, *Black Bible Chronicles, Book One: From Genesis to the Promised Land* (New York: African American Family Press, 1993), 99–100. Used by permission.

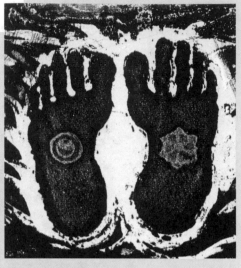

Paul Koli, *The Burning Bush*, detail, as reproduced in *The Bible Through Asian Eyes*, ed. Masao Takenaka and Ron O'Grady (Auckland, New Zealand: Pace Publishing in association with the Asian Christian Art Association, 1991), 41. Used by permission of the Asian Christian Art Association.

God asks,
   "Whom shall I send?"
God calls,
   "Come, I will send you."

Plant your feet

Go down Moses,

way down in Egypt land.

Tell ol' Pharaoh,

"Let my people go!"

African American Spiritual

I feel God calling me to . . .

....
....
....
....
....

Festival of Freedom

Meichel Pressman, *The Seder*, 1950, watercolor on paper, gift of Dr. Henry Pressman, The Jewish Museum, New York, N.Y. (Art Resource, N.Y.). Used by permission.

This day shall be a day of remembrance for you. You shall celebrate it as a festival to God; throughout your generations you shall observe it as a perpetual ordinance.

Exodus 12:14

In every generation,
each man
is obliged to see himself
as though
he went out of Egypt.

In every generation,
every woman
is obliged to see herself
as though she went out from Egypt. . . .

We were slaves unto Pharaoh in Egypt. And the Shekinah brought us from there with a mighty hand and outstretched arm. If the Holy One had not brought out our daughters and sons, our children's children, we would still have been slaves to Pharaoh in Egypt. Although if we were all wise, all sensible, experienced, understanding of the Torah, it would still be our duty to tell of the departure from Egypt, and the more one tells of the departure from Egypt, the more she is to be praised.

E. M. Broner, "The Women's Haggadah," in *The Telling* (San Francisco: HarperCollins Publishers, 1993), 76, 193.

A Seder is a special meal eaten the first night of Passover. This family is gathered around the table for their Passover Seder.

Why do you think Passover is an important event to remember and celebrate?

If you had experienced the Exodus or the Passover, what difference might it have made when you faced other difficult times?

God liberates us!
God delivers!

Meichel Pressman, *The Seder,* detail, 1950, watercolor on paper, gift of Dr. Henry Pressman, The Jewish Museum, New York, N.Y. (Art Resource, N.Y.). Used by permission.

Adir Hu

1 A - dir hu, a - dir hu, yiv-
1 God of might, God of right,
2 We en - slaved thus were saved

neh vei - to b' - ka - rov, bim - hei - ra
we would bow be - fore you, sing your praise
through God's might ap - pear - ing, so we pray

bim - hei - ra b' - ya - mei - nu, b' - ka - rov Eil b' - nei,
in these days, cel - e - brate your glo - ry, as we hear
for the day when we shall be hear - ing free - dom's call

eil b' - nei, b'nei veit - cha b' - ka - rov.
year by year, free - dom's won - drous sto - ry.
reach - ing all, the peo - ple's God re - ver - ing.

From Howard I. Bogot and Robert J. Orkand, A Children's Haggadah (New York: Central Conference of American Rabbis, 1994), 70. Used by permission.

10

Through the Sea

Then Moses stretched out his hand over the sea. God drove the sea back by a strong east wind all night, and turned the sea into dry land; the waters were divided. The Israelites went into the sea on dry ground, the waters forming a wall for them on their right and on their left.

Exodus 14:21–22

William Baziotes,
The Beach, 1955,
The Whitney Museum
of American Art,
New York, N.Y.
Used by permission.

The waves in William Baziotes's painting are reminiscent of flames. Both the light of a flame and the waves of the sea remind faithful people of God's liberating actions during the Exodus from Egypt.

A Meditation for Lighting a Candle

We light a candle to remind us of freedom,
one light that reminds us that not all are free.
A candle lighted, extinguished, and lighted again.
The hope of freedom shines bright, falters, and is rekindled anew.

We light a candle to remind us of freedom.
Our celebration is not complete when freedom is not complete.
With all who are enslaved, oppressed, victimized,
we wait for deliverance.

We light a candle to remind us of freedom.
One light to remind us of our job
to witness and work for freedom for all,
to join God in the work that remains to be done.

this great move- ment

If you were to join this great movement of people toward freedom, where would you walk? Which of those pictured here would be your closest traveling companions?

Commission

Leader: Those who journey toward freedom never journey alone.

All: Sing a new song. Sing a song of freedom!

Leader: To victims of injustice, God brings action for change.

All: Sing a new song. Sing a song of freedom!

Leader: To the downhearted, God brings a promise of deliverance.

All: Sing a new song. Sing a song of freedom!

Leader: To a world filled with oppression, God brings the light of hope.

All: Sing a new song. Sing a song of freedom!

Leader: To all who suffer wrongly, God brings change.

All: Sing a new song. Sing a song of freedom!

Leader: Go forth with a song and God travels with you.

All: Sing a new song. Sing a song of freedom!

Shalom of Safed, *The Exodus with the Pillar of Fire*, 1967, as reproduced in *Images from the Bible: The Words of Elie Wiesel, the paintings of Shalom of Safed* (New York: The Overlook Press, 1980), 107. Paintings © 1980 by Shalom of Safed. Used by permission.

Rain Down Bread

The whole congregation of the Israelites complained against Moses and Aaron in the wilderness. Then God said to Moses, "I am going to rain bread from heaven for you, and each day the people shall go out and gather enough for that day. In that way I will test them, whether they will follow my instruction or not."

Exodus 16:2, 4

A Child Writes from Sarajevo

In my dreams, I walk among the ruins
of the old part of town
looking for a bit of stale bread.

My mother and I inhale the fumes of gunpowder.
I imagine it to be the smell of pies, cakes, and kebab.

A shot rings out from a nearby hill. We hurry.
Though it's only nine o'clock, we might be hurrying
toward a grenade marked "ours."

An explosion rings out in the street of dignity.
Many people are wounded—
sisters, brothers, mothers, fathers.

I reach out to touch a trembling, injured hand.
I touch death itself.

Terrified, I realize this is not a dream.
It is just another day in Sarajevo.

Edina, 12, from Sarajevo, in *I Dream of Peace: Images of War by Children of Former Yugoslavia* (New York: HarperCollins, 1994), 47. © 1994 UNICEF. Used by permission of HarperCollins Publishers, Inc.

Stained Glass Window, *Manna from Heaven*,
Great Malvern Priory, Worcester, Great Britain
(Bridgeman/Art Resource, N.Y.)
Used by permission.

Look at the expressions on the faces of the people in this window. What do you think is going through their minds as manna rains down on them from the sky?

God promises assurance in times of hunger and need.

Assurance

God promises assurance in times of hunger.
Those who are lonely will not be abandoned.
Genuine meaning can be found in the midst of suffering.
Grief can bring healing.
Death does not have the final word.

God promises assurance in times of hunger.
Wells can be dug and fresh water poured forth.
Seeds can be planted and nourishing grains produced.
Hope springs anew.
God's love can show through human actions.

God promises assurance in times of hunger.
In the midst of confusion, new possibilities are discovered.
In times of despair, new light shines forth.
Hope blossoms.
Love is victorious.

Ted Huffman

As the Grains of Wheat

As the grains of wheat once scattered on the hill
were gathered into one to become our bread;
so may all your people from all the ends of the earth
be gathered into one in you.

Tell the glorious deeds

Jacob Lawrence, *Harriet Hear Tell*, in *Harriet Tubman and the Promised Land*
(New York: Simon and Schuster, 1968), Used by permission.

We will not hide them from their children; we will tell to the coming generations the glorious deeds of God, and God's might, and the wonders that God has done.

Psalm 78:4

God worked glorious deeds through Harriet Tubman's life. The story of Moses and the Exodus learned as a child inspired her. Over a ten-year period, she helped over two hundred slaves find freedom through the Underground Railroad, a secret network that led runaway slaves to safety.

I can only explain my own life and the events of the times in which I've lived in the context of faith—a biblical faith that continues to see the hand of God working in the affairs of the children of creation. This is a simple proclamation of my understanding of life. My life has unfolded around me in ways that fill me with awe and wonder. . . . The testimony of men and women down through the ages can help us to discover or discern a spiritual direction for our lives.

Andrew Young, *A Way Out of No Way*
(Nashville: Thomas Nelson Publishers, 1994), 2.

Stories help us touch the eternal.

MOYERS: Myths are stories of our search through the ages for the truth, for meaning, for significance. We need to tell our story and to understand our story. We all need to understand death and to cope with death, and we all need help in our passages from birth to life and then to death. We need for life to signify, to touch the eternal, to understand the mysterious, to find out who we are.

CAMPBELL: People say that what we're all seeking is meaning for life. I don't think that's what we're really seeking. I think what we're seeking is an experience of being alive, so that our life experience on the purely physical plane will have resonance within our own innermost being and reality, so that we actually feel the rapture of being alive.

Joseph Campbell and Bill Moyers, *The Power of Myth,* ed. Betty Sue Flowers (New York: Doubleday, 1988), 5. Used by permission of Doubleday, a division of Bantam Dell Doubleday Publishing Group, Inc.

Young aborigines listen to stories to learn who they are.

Ainslie Roberts, *The Storyteller,* 1976, as reproduced in *Ainsley Roberts and the Dreamtime* (Richmond, Victoria, South Australia: J.M. Dent Pty, 1988). Used by permission.

Our faith draws us together this day.
Let us trust enough to open our ears and our hearts.
 We have heard of God's miracles in other times;
 our ancestors have kept the story alive for us.
Give ear, all people, to God's word for today.
Taste the bounty of God's blessing here and now.
 We long for a faith that makes sense for today.
 We want to keep the story alive for new generations.
God's revelation is for all people, near and far.
God is waiting to communicate with you and me.
 May God have mercy on us and all people.
 Surely God's will shall be made known to us.

Lavon Bayler, *Fresh Winds of the Spirit, Book 2: Liturgical Resources for Year A* (Cleveland, Ohio: Pilgrim Press, 1992), 120. Used by permission.

Tadao Tanaka, *The Ten Commandments*, in *The Bible Through Asian Eyes*, ed.
Masao Takenaka and Ron O'Grady (Auckland, New Zealand: Pace Publishing in
association with the Asian Christian Art Association, 1991). Used by permission.

You Shall . . .

I am the Sovereign your God, who
brought you out of the land of Egypt,
out of the house of slavery; you shall
have no other gods before me.

Exodus 20:2–3

*Look at the actions of the people
in the picture. What is the focus
of the crowd? Why do you suppose
some people are smiling?*

What is my . . .

. . . Duty

Psalm 19:7–11

The law of God is perfect, reviving the soul;
the testimony of God is sure, making wise the simple;
the precepts of God are right, rejoicing the heart;
the commandment of God is clear, enlightening the eyes;
the fear of God is pure, enduring forever;
the ordinances of God are true and righteous altogether.
More to be desired are they than gold, even much fine gold;
sweeter also than honey and drippings of the honeycomb.
Moreover by them is your servant warned;
    in keeping them there is great reward.

Inclusive Language Psalms: Readings for Years A, B, and C
(New York: The Pilgrim Press, 1987), 14. Used by permission.

. . . Devotion

. . . Covenant

. . . to God?

Grade 4 at St. Francis Xavier
School, *Moses Quilt*, 1994,
45 West High Street, Gettysburg
PA 17325. Used by permission.

This quilt was created by fourth-grade students at St. Francis Xavier School in Gettysburg, Pennsylvania, as a way of learning the stories about Moses. After hanging in the local church for a few months, the quilt was sent to a Franciscan mission in Kenya.

I Shall

A Prayer

Come, fulfill the law in us, dear God.
Give us wisdom and strength to accept your law
      as a blessing.
Give us courage and devotion to follow your law
      as our duty and covenant with you.
Hear our silent prayers now as we ask for your help
      in following these commandments.
      [Pause for silent prayers.]
God, go with us from this place now,
      and remain our blessing, our peace, and the
      Word that dwells among us.
Amen.

How will you do this?

1.

2.

3.

MANY CALLED, FEW CHOSEN

Diego Rivera, *Dance in Tehuantepec*, 1928, private collection, courtesy of Sotheby's, New York, N.Y. Used by permission.

Jesus said, "The dominion of heaven may be compared to a king who gave a wedding banquet for his son. He sent his slaves to call those who had been invited to the wedding banquet, but they would not come. For many are called, but few are chosen."

Matthew 22:2–3, 14

Just as these dancers put on special clothing to perform, Christians are called to put on God's expectations to live faithful lives. How can you dress yourself for God's dominion?

Only those who let themselves be
    transformed here
  those willing to become new people
  to "put on Christ"
  and become a "new creation"
in the unimaginable patterns of the
    God of life:
. . . [are] wedding guests in living
    garments,
fully engaged in God's feast of life.

Susan A. Blain, "A Preaching Dress Sermon,"
James Memorial Chapel, Union Theological
Seminary, New York City, October 16, 1987.
Used by permission.

He dressed me. My Lord, he put new rags on me, and I am a wonder beside him.

Walter Wangerin, Jr., *Ragman and Other
Cries of Faith* (San Francisco: Harper &
Row, 1984), 6. Copyright © 1984 by
Walter Wangerin, Jr. Used by permission of
HarperCollins Publishers, Inc.

Rembrandt Harmensz van Rijn, *The Parable of the Unworthy Wedding Guest*, The Albertina Museum, Vienna, Austria. Used by permission.

"When the king came in to look at the guests, he saw someone who had no wedding garment; and the king said, 'Friend, how did you get in here without a wedding garment?' And the guest was speechless. Then the king said to the attendants, 'Let the guest be bound hand and foot and cast into the night.'"

Matthew 22:11–13, *An Inclusive-Language Lectionary: Readings for Year A*, rev. ed. (New York: The Pilgrim Press, 1986), 230. Used by permission.

Who shall ascend into the hill of the Lord? or who shall stand in his holy place? There is no one but us. There is no one to send, nor a clean hand, nor a pure heart on the face of the earth, nor in the earth, but only us, a generation comforting ourselves with the notion that we have come at an awkward time, that our innocent fathers are all dead—as if innocence had ever been—and our children busy and troubled, and we ourselves unfit, not yet ready, having each of us chosen wrongly, made a false start, failed, yielded to impulse and the tangled comfort of pleasures, and grown exhausted, unable to seek the thread, weak, and involved. But there is no one but us. There never has been. There have been generations which remembered, and generations which forgot; there has never been a generation of whole men and women who lived well for even one day. Yet some have imagined well, with honesty and art, the detail of such a life, and have described it with grace.

Annie Dillard, *Holy the Firm* (New York: Harper & Row, 1977). Copyright © 1977 by Annie Dillard. Used by permission of HarperCollins Publishers, Inc.

WHAT'S EXPECTED OF ME?

Belonging to God

Jesus said, "Show me the coin used for the tax." And they brought him a denarius. Then Jesus said to them, "Whose head is this, and whose title?" They answered, "The emperor's." Then Jesus said to them, "Give therefore to the emperor the things that are the emperor's and to God the things that are God's." When they heard this, they were amazed.

Matthew 22:19–22a

Titian, *The Tribute Money*, The National Gallery, London, England. Used by permission.

Titian accents the drama of the story by his use of light, which throws the faces in the painting into relief. Look at the range of expressions on those faces. How do the two characters seem to be reacting to Jesus?

It is as if [Jesus] had said: God, like Caesar, demands from you the impression of [God's] own image. Just as you repay his coinage to Caesar, so return your soul to God, shining and stamped with the light of [God's] countenance.

St. Augustine, *St. Augustine on the Psalms,* trans. Dame Scholastica Hebin and Dame Fekucutas Corrigan (New York: Newman Press, n.d.), adapted. Used by permission of Paulist Press

Thus says YAHWEH who made you,
    who formed you in the womb and will help you:
Do not fear . . .
For I will pour water on the thirsty land,
    and streams on the dry ground;
I will pour my spirit upon your descendants,
    and my blessing on your offspring.
They shall spring up like a green tamarisk,
    like willows by flowing streams.
This one will say, "I am God's,"
. . . yet another will write on the hand, "YAHWEH'S,"
    and adopt the name of Israel.

Isaiah 44:2–5

[God] coined us
in [God's] image. . . .
We are [God's] money,
and we should be spent. . . .
Money should circulate,
we should circulate;
money should go from hand to hand,
we should go from hand to hand; . . .
money should be used,
we should be used; . . .
money is going to be worn,
we should be going to be worn.

We should be spent,
we are coins,
God is trying to use us,
to pay off our debts,
to pay off the debts we owe each other
here on earth. . . .

Let us risk being used,
and we will be increased,
and the end will be glory. . . .

Joseph G. Donders, *Jesus the Stranger:
Reflections on the Gospel* (Maryknoll, N.Y.:
Orbis Books, 1978). Used by permission of
Joseph G. Donders.

Whose are you?

At Home with God

Charles E. Burchfield, *Six O'Clock*, detail, Everson Museum of Art, Syracuse, N.Y. Used by permission.

¹ God, you have been our dwelling place in all generations. ² Before the mountains were brought forth, or ever you had formed the earth and the world, from everlasting to everlasting you are God.

Psalm 90:1–2

Psalm 90:3–6, 13–17

3 You turn us back to dust,
   and say, "Turn back, you mortals."
4 For a thousand years in your sight
   are like yesterday when it is past,
   or like a watch in the night.
5 You sweep them away; they are like a dream,
   like grass that is renewed in the morning;
6 in the morning it flourishes and is renewed;
   in the evening it fades and withers.
13 Turn, O God! How long?
   Have compassion on your servants!
14 Satisfy us in the morning with your steadfast love,
   so that we may rejoice and be glad all our days.
15 Make us glad as many days as you have afflicted us,
   and as many years as we have seen evil.
16 Let your work be manifest to your servants,
   and your glorious power to their children.
17 Let the favor of the sovereign God be upon us,
   and prosper for us the work of our hands—
   O prosper the work of our hands!

What are the characteristics of your ideal home?

What are the hazards and trials from which an ideal home protects you?

Charles E. Burchfield, *Six O'Clock*, Everson Museum of Art, Syracuse, N.Y. Used by permission.

All that matters is to be at one with **the living God** to be a creature in the house of **the God of Life....**

D. H. Lawrence, "Pax," in *The Complete Poems of D. H. Lawrence*, ed. Vivian de Sola Pinto and F. Warren Roberts (New York: Viking Press, 1964), 1:153. Used by permission.

You Are Mine

I will come to you in the silence,
I will lift you from all your fear.
You will hear my voice, I claim you as my choice,
be still and know I am here.

I am hope for all who are hopeless,
I am eyes for all who long to see.
In the shadows of the night, I will be your light,
come and rest in me.

I am strength for all the despairing,
healing for the ones who dwell in shame.
All the blind will see, the lame will all run free,
and all will know my name.

I am the Word that leads all to freedom,
I am the peace the world cannot give.
I will call your name, embracing all your pain,
stand up, now walk, and live!

Do not be afraid, I am with you.
I have called you each by name.
Come and follow me, I will bring you home;
I love you and you are mine.

From Table to Town

Andrew Wyeth, *Christina's World*, 1948, tempera on gesso panel, 32 ¼ x 47 ¾," The Museum of Modern Art, New York, N.Y. Purchase. Photograph © 1996, The Museum of Modern Art. Used by permission.

Some wandered in desert wastes, finding no way to an inhabited town; hungry and thirsty, their soul fainted within them. Then they cried to God in their trouble, and God delivered them from their distress. And there God lets the hungry live, and they establish a town to live in.

Psalm 107:4–6, 36

There is a sense of yearning in Christina as she looks toward home. What ways do you yearn to have your needs met?

**O God of encounters,
may each of us
in his desert
detect a sign of your presence. . . .**

Pierre Talec, *Bread in the Desert,* trans. Edmond Bonin
(New York: Newman Press, 1973), 100. Used by permission.

"Those who drink of the water that I will give them will never be thirsty."

John 4:14

Lord,
help us find the well
where you await us
at every stage of our lives.
And we shall set out again,
thirsting, at last,
for none but the living water
which you have promised us. Amen.

Pierre Talec, *Bread in the Desert*, trans.
Edmond Bonin (New York: Newman Press,
1973), 83. Used by permission.

How might God use community
to respond to people's needs?

What needs do you see being
met in this painting?

Manuscript Illumination, *Depiction of a Medieval Town (August: Corn Harvest)*, c. 1500, *Golf Book of Hours*,
MS. Add 24098, f.25v., British Library, London, England (Bridgeman/Art Resource, N.Y.).
Used by permission.

Choose This Day

Gotta Serve Somebody

You may be an ambassador to England or France,
You may like to gamble, you might like to dance.
You may be the heavyweight champion of the world,
You might be a socialite with a long string of pearls.

But you're gonna have to serve somebody, yes indeed,
You're gonna have to serve somebody.
Well it may be the devil, or it may be the Lord,
But you're gonna have to serve somebody. . . .

Might like to wear cotton, you might like to wear silk.
Might like to drink whiskey, might like to drink milk.
You might like to eat caviar, you might like to eat bread.
You might be sleeping on the floor, sleeping in a king-sized bed.

But you're gonna have to serve somebody, yes indeed,
You're gonna have to serve somebody.
Well it may be the devil, or it may be the Lord,
But you're gonna have to serve somebody. . . .

Bob Dylan, *Gotta Serve Somebody*, Copyright © 1979 Special Rider Music.
Used by permission.

Joshua said, "Now if you are unwilling to serve God, choose this day whom you will serve, whether the gods your ancestors served in the region beyond the River or the gods of the Amorites in whose land you are living; but as for me and my household, we will serve God."

Joshua 24:15

Sandra Jorgensen, *Roads*, Elmhurst, Illinois. Used by permission.

How do you know what road to choose?

What difference does it make when you choose one road over another?

Whom or what do you serve?

To whom do you give your devotion?

Treë, *Signature*, Photogratree, 285 Mott Street, Apt. A17, New York NY 10012-3430. Used by permission.

Watershed

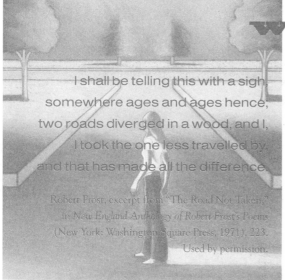

I shall be telling this with a sigh,
somewhere ages and ages hence;
two roads diverged in a wood, and I,
I took the one less travelled by,
and that has made all the difference.

Robert Frost, excerpt from "The Road Not Taken,"
in *New England Anthology of Robert Frost's Poems*
(New York: Washington Square Press, 1971), 223.
Used by permission.

Search me, O God, and know my heart. Lead me in the way everlasting.

Psalm 139:23a, 24b

Thought I knew my mind like the back of my hand,
The gold and the rainbow, but nothing panned out as I planned.
And they say only milk and honey's gonna make your soul satisfied!
Well I better learn how to swim
Cause the crossing is chilly and wide.
Twisted guardrail on the highway, broken glass on the cement.
A ghost of someone's tragedy
How recklessly my time has been spent.
And they say that it's never too late, but you don't get any younger!
Well I better learn how to starve the emptiness
And feed the hunger.

> *Refrain: Up on the watershed, standing at the fork in the road*
> *You can stand there and agonize*
> *Till your agony's your heaviest load.*
> *You'll never fly as the crow flies, get used to a country mile.*
> *When you're learning to face the path at your pace*
> *Every choice is worth your while.*

Well there's always retrospect to light a clearer path
Every five years or so I look back on my life
And I have a good laugh.
You start at the top, go full circle round
Catch a breeze, take a spill—
But ending up where I started again makes me wanna stand still,
Stepping on a crack, breaking up and looking back.
Every tree limb overhead just seems to sit and wait
Until every step you take becomes a twist of fate.

Emily Saliers, *Watershed*, copyright 1990, Godhap Music (BMI), Virgin Songs, Inc.
Used by permission.

According to Ability

Jesus said, "For it is as if someone, going on a journey, summoned slaves and entrusted property to them; giving to one five talents, to another two, to another one, all according to their ability; and went away. After a long time the master of those slaves came and settled accounts with them."

Matthew 25:14–15, 19

Glen Strock, *Parable of the Talents*, Dixon, N.M. Used by permission.

How does this painting tell the story of Jesus' parable of the talents? Are you one who saves your talents or risks using them?

"If I were the Creator," Nathan said, "most of all, I'd want my creatures to live every minute of their life, not be so afraid of doing something wrong that they failed to savor the feast I'd prepared for them. I'd want my people to plant, and swim, and taste, and see, and play. As the sunsets' and the rainbows' creator, I'd love these purple and acid-greens you've painted this room, and I would be glad you risked loving."

Grant Spradling, *End of the Road*, unpublished. Used by permission.

Talents God Has Given Me . . .

© Bill Barrett. Used by permission.

Invest your talents.

STONE SOUP:
An Old Tale

> This is a communal kitchen in a refugee camp on the border of Honduras and El Salvador. As in the story below, everybody contributed the food they had. Combined with the food the camp received from nonprofit agencies and the United Nations, there was enough for everyone to eat.

In the popular legend of Stone Soup, a young wanderer traveled throughout the countryside. He stopped in one small village, hoping for a place to rest and a bite to eat. But the villagers had had a hard year. With losses from a war and a poor harvest, they adopted an "every family for itself" policy. Each family hid all its food, hoarding it so no one would find it.

So the wanderer came up with a creative idea to get the people to share. He announced that he knew how to make a soup from stones! The villagers were intrigued and came to watch. The wanderer dropped a large stone into a steaming pot of water. He then stirred and stirred, brought the ladle to his nose, and sniffed. Then he declared, "It's wonderful! Does anyone have any salt? Just a small amount would help this rich broth!" Slowly the villagers began to offer odds and ends of food for the boiling pot. Soon the whole village had contributed to the soup—which smelled wonderful! Tables were set up in the village square, and the whole village shared in a feast to which everyone had contributed. Community was fostered, no one was isolated anymore, and people helped one another.

And the young wanderer left with a bellyful—and as a community hero.

French Traditional Folktale

The Least of These

Jesus said that the last shall be **first** and the first shall be **last.** Who among the "least" **can you help** to make first?

"Truly I tell you, just as you did it to one of the least of these who are members of my family, you did it to me."

Matthew 25:40b

Mona Reeder, *Hau Li Eating Lunch by himself*, from *The Daily Republic*, Suisun City, CA, in *The Best of Photojournalism #18: The Year in Pictures, 1993*, National Press Photographers' Association, University of Missouri School of Journalism, 1993. Used by permission.

Another Day in Paradise

1.
She calls out to the man on the street,
"Sir, can you help me?"
"It's cold and I've nowhere to sleep,
is there somewhere you can tell me?"

2.
He walks on, doesn't look back,
He pretends he can't hear her,
Starts to whistle as he crosses the street,
Seems embarrassed to be there.

Chorus:
Oh think twice, 'cos it's another day for
you and me in paradise,
oh think twice, 'cos it's another day for you,
you and me in paradise.
Just think about it.
Oh Lord, is there nothing more anybody can do,
oh Lord, there must be something you can say.

3.
She calls out to the man on the street,
He can see she's been crying,
She's got blisters on the soles of her feet,
She can't walk, but she's trying.

4.
You can tell from the lines on her face,
You can see that she's been there.
Probably been moved on from every place,
'Cos she didn't fit in there.

As You Did It to One of the Least of These My Brethren

O God, who is old, and lives on fifty dollars a month, in one crummy room and can't get outside,
Help us to see you.

O God, who is fifteen and in the sixth grade,
Help us to see you.

O God, who is three and whose belly aches in hunger,
Help us to see you, as you have seen us in Jesus Christ our Lord.

O God, who sleeps in a bed with your four brothers and sisters, and who cries and no one hears you,
Help us to touch you.

O God, who has no place to sleep tonight except an abandoned car, an alley or deserted building,
Help us to touch you.

O God, who is uneducated, unskilled, unwanted, and unemployed,
Help us to touch you, as you have touched us in Jesus Christ our Lord.

. . .

O God, who is chased by the cops, who sits in jail for seven months with no charges brought, waiting for the Grand Jury and no money for bail,
Help us to know you.

. . .

O God, who is unorganized, and without strength to change your world, your city, your neighborhood,
Help us to join you.

O God, who is fed up with it all and who is determined to do something, who is organizing people for power to change the world,
Help us to join you, as you have joined us in Jesus Christ our Lord. Amen.

Robert W. Castle, Jr., in *The Wideness of God's Mercy*, ed. Jeffrey W. Rowthorn (Minneapolis: Seabury Press, 1985), 2:164–65. Used by permission.

"I will seek the lost, and I will bring back the strayed, and I will bind up the injured, and I will strengthen the weak, but the fat and the strong I will destroy. I will feed them with justice."

Ezekiel 34:16

Christ Enthroned with Angels, mosaic, 6th century, S. Apollinare Nuovo, Ravenna, Italy (Alinari/Art Resource, N.Y.). Used by permission.

" . . . you did it to me."

Keep Awake

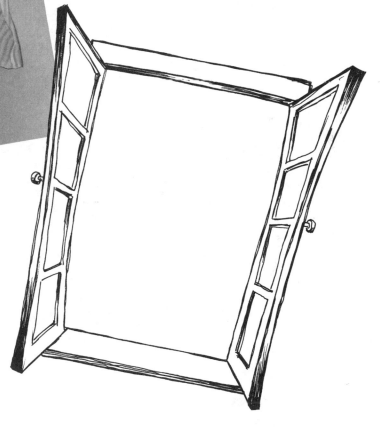

"Therefore, keep awake—for you do not know when the owner of the house will come, in the evening, or at midnight, or at cockcrow, or at dawn, or else the owner may find you asleep when coming suddenly. And what I say to you I say to all: Keep awake."

Mark 13:35–37

Salvador Dali, *Girl Standing at the Window*, 1925, Museo d'Arts Contemporanea, Madrid, Spain. (Bridgeman/Art Resource, N.Y.). Used by permission.

Salvador Dali painted this picture of his sister at a window.

**What do you imagine about her story?
What promise lies ahead of her?**

Among the earliest hearers of the Gospel of Mark were Jewish and Gentile Christians who were suffering and being persecuted because of their faith. Mark's words were written, in part, to encourage those early Christians. Followers of Christ sometimes suffer. They are always called to serve. Christians need to keep awake in every generation in order to respond to the call to service and to the opportunity to follow Jesus.

Put **yourself** in the picture

Keep Awake, Be Always Ready

Words: Arthur G. Clyde, 1993   Tune: WACHET AUF, by Philipp Nicolai, 1599

1 Keep a - wake, be al - ways rea - dy, God's time ap - proach - es
2 Rise and shine for One is com - ing whose love will quench all

sure and stea - dy, God's strength will keep your heart from blame.
na - ture's thirst - ing to be made whole for - ev - er more.

Clouds, the Spir - it's light con - ceal - ing, dis - perse, God's pur - est
On that day to end all weep - ing, death's swords trans - formed to

light re - veal - ing; cre - a - tion will its Sov - ereign name. Dry
tools of reap - ing, the God of might will mer - cy pour. In -

branch - es burst forth green, God's ad - vent signs are
car - nate, God ap - pears em - brac - ing all our

seen: Hal - le - lu - jah! Christ's judg - ment won, God's
tears: Hal - le - lu - jah! God's maj - es - ty e -

will be done; God's new do - min - ion thus be - gun.
ter - nal - ly re - vealed to set the cos - mos free.

> **Sober watchfulness is the partner of joyous expectancy as believers anticipate the promise of God's coming.**
>
> Paul Hammer,
> "The Background Word"

Salvador Dali, *Girl Standing at the Window*, detail, 1925,
Museo d'Arts Contemporanea, Madrid, Spain.
(Bridgeman/Art Resource, N.Y.). Used by permission.

get ready

"See, I am sending my messenger ahead of you, who will prepare your way; the voice of one crying out in the wilderness: 'Prepare the way of the Sovereign, make straight the Sovereign's paths.'"

Mark 1:2b–3

Repent! Change! repent! repent!

Pieter Bruegel, the Elder, *Sermon of St. John the Baptist*, 1566, Szépmùvézeti Múzeum, Budapest, Hungary. Used by permission.

Notice the positions of the people in the crowd. Many seem mesmerized by John, several are looking away from him, a few are talking amongst themselves, and at least one is up in a tree in order to see better. Put yourself in the picture. Where would you be?

change!

The Wilderness

The wilderness
he preached
in was his own country.
A wilderness
not coming
from the hands of God
but a jungle
caused by innumerable
human decisions
that were
     wrong,
     shortsighted,
     and selfish.
Decisions that have created havoc
in the lives
of the many.
     It was in that
     jungle
     that John preached
     and baptized.

As long as we think
about John
like that
—preaching
in his own country
two thousand years ago—
his preaching
remains distant
and very far away.
Let us try
to get that wilderness
and also John's word
nearer home,
so that it can cut us
to the bone.
Let us speak
about the wilderness
in which we live.
And let us think
not only of sin
but of the world
we are accustomed to.

Pieter Bruegel, the Elder, *Sermon of St. John the Baptist*, detail, 1566, Szépmùvézeti Múzeum, Budapest, Hungary. Used by permission.

Joseph G. Donders, *The Jesus Community: Reflections on the Gospels for the B-Cycle* (Maryknoll, N.Y.: Orbis Books, 1981), 12–13. Used by permission.

If John were alive today, what messages would he shout from our wilderness?

Good NEWS COMING

For as the earth brings
forth its shoots, and as a
garden causes what is
sown in it to spring up,
so the Sovereign God
will cause righteousness
and praise to spring up
before all the nations.

Isaiah 61:11

Minnie Evans, Museum at Michigan State University,
East Lansing, Mich. Used by permission.

Earth teach me stillness
    as the grasses are stilled with light.
Earth teach me suffering
    as old stones suffer with memory.
Earth teach me humility
    as blossoms are humble with beginning.
Earth teach me caring
    as the mother who secures her young.
Earth teach me courage
    as the tree which stands all alone.
Earth teach me limitation
    as the ant which crawls on the ground.
Earth teach me freedom
    as the eagle which soars in the sky.
Earth teach me resignation
    as the leaves which die in the fall.
Earth teach me regeneration
    as the seed which rises in the spring.
Earth teach me to forget myself
    as melted snow forgets its life.
Earth teach me to remember kindness
    as dry fields weep with rain.

"Ute Prayer," in Earth Prayers from Around the World,
    ed. Elizabeth Roberts and Elias Amidon (San Francisco:
HarperSan Francisco, 1990).

Imagine a world where righteousness
grows like summer flowers and blossoms
to celebrate God's presence. May you not
only imagine, but help to build, that world.

I Dream of
PEACE

Senad Gubelic, *Child with Gun*, as reproduced in
*I Dream of Peace: Images of War by Children of Former
Yugoslavia* (New York: HarperCollins Publishers, 1994), 76.
Used by permission of HarperCollins Publishers, Inc.

**This child has seen his world torn apart
by war. Imagine his story. What do you
think has happened to him? What is
needed to enable him to celebrate God's
coming with praise and righteousness?
How could older people—like you—help?**

Excerpted from *Children as Teachers
of Peace*, ed. Gerald G. Jampolsky (Berkeley:
Celestial Arts, 1982), 52. Copyright © 1982
by Foundation for Spiritual Alternatives.
Used by permission of
Celestial Arts, Berkeley CA.

The child who sketched this picture has a vision of peace.
What do you guess are the
differences and similarities
between this child and the
one pictured above?
What does your vision of
peace look like?

Christine O'Keeffe
Age 12

Peace is when people do not fight. There
is no prejudice. And all people join as one,
each person their very best self.

Greetings, Favored One!

The angel Gabriel came to Mary and said, "Greetings, favored one! God is with you." But she was much perplexed by the words and pondered what sort of greeting this might be. The angel said to her, "Do not be afraid, Mary, for you have found favor with God. And now, you will conceive in your womb and bear a son, and you will name him Jesus."

Luke 1:28–31

We know you, God, because you act in the world.

We know you because you act in our lives.

But sometimes we do not know that it is you;

Sometimes we do not see your actions.

Help us to see you when you act.

Help us to recognize you in our own lives.

Help us to respond as did Mary,

"Here I am, God. Here I am."

Barbara Cooney, in *Spirit Child: A Story of the Nativity*, trans. John Bierhorst (New York: Mulberry Books, 1984), 6–7. Used by permission.

This is one artist's idea of how the conversation between Mary and Gabriel might have happened. How do you imagine it?

The mystery of God's action

Explore the face of Mary.

Love Song

Words and music: James K. Manley, 1980

1 And Mar-y, she sang a love song, Mar-y, she sang a
2 And Mar-y, she sang a love song, Mar-y, she sang a
3 And Je-sus, he sang a love song, Je-sus, he sang a
4 And Je-sus, he sang a love song, Je-sus, he sang a
5 And Je-sus, he sang a love song, Je-sus, he sang a
6 Ev-ery-bod-y come sing the love song, ev-ery-bod-y come sing the

love song, and Mar-y, she sang a love song, she sang a
love song, and Mar-y, she sang a love song, she sang a
love song, and Je-sus, he sang a love song, he sang a
love song, and Je-sus, he sang a love song, he sang a
love song, and Je-sus, he sang a love song, he sang a
love song, ev-ery-bod-y come sing the love song, — sing the

love song to her ba - by._____
love song to her ba - by._____
love song to his mam - ma._____
love song to the fish-er - men._____
love song to ev-ery-bod - y._____
love song of___ Je - sus._____ *Last time, end*

1 Lamp light on the sta - ble walls, sha-dows in the
2 Twelve years old and fin-ally found, talk-ing in the
3 Thir-ty years, and by the shore, "Tell me what you're
4 Thir-ty-three, and through the pain Je-sus sang it
5 Morn-ing time and by the sea the song he sang

cat-tle stalls, a song of love on a mam-ma's words, she
tem-ple grounds, — "Son, how could you do this thing?" —
fish-ing for; — leave your nets and come a-long, and
once a-gain; — stark a-gainst the fall-ing sky the
comes to me. I heard it first when I was young and

To beginning

sings the song_____ which she first heard.
"Mam - ma, you_____ taught me to sing."
I'll teach you_____ my fish-ing song!"
song went up_____ on a sin-gle cry.
now I want_____ to sing the song.

Copyright © 1980 by James K. Manley, 434 Ives Terrace, Sunnyvale, CA 94087.

All rights reserved. Used by permission for United Church Press.

Top:
Barbara Cooney,
detail, in *Spirit Child:
A Story of the Nativity*,
trans. John Bierhorst (New York: Mulberry
Books, 1984), 6–7. Used by permission.

Middle: Ethan Hubbard, *Young Woman of
Costura, Guatemala*, detail, as reproduced in
Ethan Hubbard, *Straight to the Heart: Children
of the World* (Chelsea, Vt.: Craftsbury
Common Books, 1992). Used by permission
of the photographer.

Bottom: Henry O. Tanner, *The Annunciation*,
detail, 1898, W. P. Wilstach Collection, The
Philadelphia Museum of Art, Philadelphia, Pa.
Used by permission.

The Wise Ones

It had been revealed to Simeon by the Holy Spirit that he would not see death before he had seen God's Messiah. There was also a prophet, Anna. She was of a great age. She came, and began to praise God and to speak about the child to all who were looking for the redemption of Jerusalem.

Luke 2:26, 36a, 38

Think about Anna and Simeon.

Do you know any such people—

wise and full of faith?

Song of Simeon (Nunc Dimittis)

Holy One, now let your servant go in peace;

your word has been fulfilled;

my own eyes have seen the salvation which you

have prepared

>**in the sight of every people;**

A light to reveal you to the nations

>**and the glory of your people Israel.**

Rembrandt Harmensz van Rijn, *The Presentation of Christ in the Temple*, c. 1627–28, Kunsthalle, Hamburg, Germany (Kavaler/Art Resource, N.Y.). Used by permission.

Wisdom and Faith

Persons of Wisdom and Faith

Michael Freeman, *Shaker Woman*, London, England. Used by permission.

Look at the patience and care with which this woman is knitting. Does she remind you of anyone you know?

Create a Prayer for a Person of Wisdom and Faith

Select one person of wisdom and faith. Create a prayer for that person. You might want to consider including the following points in your prayer:

- thanksgiving for the life and health of the person of faith and wisdom

- an expression of gratitude for something that the person of faith and wisdom has given to the youth or to the community

- a hope for something that might yet be learned from the person of faith and wisdom

Child, Full of Grace

And from the fullness of the Child have we all received, grace upon grace. For the law was given through Moses; grace and truth came through Jesus Christ. No one has ever seen God; the only Child, who is in the bosom of God the Mother and Father, that one has made God known.

John 1:16–18

A Prayer for a Christmas Candle

Eternal God, we know that the candle that we just lit will soon be extinguished, but we pray that the love it symbolizes may burn in our hearts forever. This flame is a symbol. The reality of your grace, freely given, cannot be contained in any single object, time, or place. Your grace abounds. In this Christmas season, we pray that our awareness of your grace may be expanded and that our lives may become dwelling places for your gifts, that we may share as freely as we have received and that our lives might show your goodness to others. As you were born in Jesus in a humble stable long ago, be born in our hearts this Christmas. Amen.

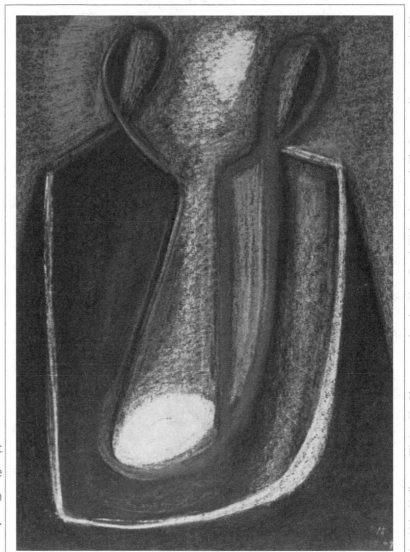

Iris Hahs-Hoffstetter, *We Saw His Glory*, as reproduced in Hans-Ruedi Weber, *Immanuel: The Coming of Jesus in Art and Bible*, (Geneva, Switzerland: WCC Publications, 1984), 111. Used by permission.

This painting is both simple and compelling. The use of a few straight and curved lines suggests intimacy; the juxtaposition of light and shadow conveys a sense of mystery. What—or who—do you think the figures are? Whose glory do you think the painter is suggesting? Who is the "we" in the title?

Grace is God's love freely given.

It does not need to be earned. It does not need to be deserved.

Grace is God's love freely given.

John Giuliani, *Hopi Virgin and Child*, Bridge Building Images, P.O. Box 1048, Burlington VT 05402. Used by permission.

No one knows what Jesus and Mary really looked like. Though they were first-century Jews from the land of Israel, they have been portrayed as people of other cultures and other eras in countless paintings. One way of understanding incarnation is to imagine Jesus and Mary as your neighbors. What do they look like in your mind's eye?

Amazing Grace

Amazing grace! How sweet the sound that saved a wretch like me.
I once was lost, but now am found, was blind, but now I see.

'Twas grace that taught my heart to fear, and grace my fears relieved.
How precious did that grace appear, the hour I first believed.

Through many dangers, toils, and snares, I have already come;
'Tis grace has brought me safe thus far, and grace will lead me home.

John Newton, 1779

American Sign Language is a language of incarnation. With hands in motion, words are made flesh through gesture.

Become

Body

44

You Are My *Beloved*

Just as Jesus was coming up out of the water, he saw
the heavens torn apart and the Spirit descending
like a dove on him. And a voice came from heaven,
"You are my Child, the Beloved; with you I am well pleased."

Mark 1:10–11

Epiphany

"Aha!"

An epiphany is a moment of insight or revelation.

An epiphany is a moment when you say,

Christ gleams with water brown with clay
from land the prophets trod.
Above while heaven's clouds give way
descends the dove of God.

Water, River, Spirit, Grace,
sweep over me, sweep over me!
Recarve the depths your fingers traced
in sculpting me.

Thomas H. Troeger, "What Ruler Wades Through
Murky Streams," Words Copyright © 1984; rev. 1993,
Oxford University Press, Inc. Used by permission.

John August Swanson, *The River,*
serigraph © 1987, Los Angeles, California.
Used by permission of the artist.

Crashing *Waters* at Creation

Words: Sylvia G. Dunstan, 1991

Tune: STUTTGART 8.7.8.7.; attr. to
Christian F. Witt (1660–1716)

1 Crash-ing wa-ters at cre-a-tion or-dered by the Spir-it's breath,
2 Part-ing wa-ter stood and trem-bled as the cap-tives passed on through,
3 Cleans-ing wa-ter once at Jor-dan closed a-round the One fore-told,
4 Liv-ing wa-ter, nev-er end-ing, quench the thirst and flood the soul.

first to wit-ness day's be-gin-ning from the bright-ness of night's death.
wash-ing off the chains of bond-age— chan-nel to a life made new.
o-pened to re-veal the glo-ry ev-er new and ev-er old.
Well-spring, Source of life e-ter-nal, drench our dry-ness, make us whole.

What transforms ordinary water into the *water of baptism*?

W. Eugene Smith photographed Tomoko's bath in a way that communicates the love and care with which she was bathed. Water does not wash away the horror of industrial pollution, but it soothes when used with love.

W. Eugene Smith, *Tomoko in Her Bath, Japan*, © Heirs of W. Eugene Smith. Used by permission of Black Star.

Here I Am!

Now God came and stood there, calling as before, "Samuel! Samuel!" And Samuel said, "Speak, for your servant is listening."

1 Samuel 3:10

Brother Eric de Saussure, *Samuel's Calling*, as reproduced in *The Taizé Picture Bible* (Lahr/Schwarzwald, Germany: Verlag Ernst Kaufmann GmbH, 1978), 109. © Atelieus et Presses de Taizé, 71250 Taizé Communauté, France. Used by permission.

Eli

The high priest with unscrupulous sons. A leader who doesn't know who will be the next to lead. A channel for God's work with the people. Eli bestowed a blessing on Hannah.

Samuel

The answer to his mother's prayers, child of Hannah and Elkanah. The one whose name literally means "the name of God," or perhaps "the one over whom the name of God is pronounced." Samuel blessed Eli by growing to love God as deeply as did Eli.

How do you picture the young Samuel?

QUIET TIME IS A GIFT FROM GOD. QUIET TIME CAN BE A GIFT TO GOD AS WELL.

A Litany of Listening

One: We offer quiet moments to you, O God.

Many: Quiet isn't silent.

One: We hear sounds.

Many: We make sounds.

One: Help us to listen to the quiet times, God.

Many: Help us to listen to you, God.

One: Quiet times aren't always easy, God.

Many: Quiet prayer demands work and practice.

One: Be patient with our practice, God.

Many: Help us to be patient with our practice as well.

One: May our quiet times help you to know us, God.

Many: May our quiet times help us to know you. Amen.

Listen

Listen with the ear of your heart

And hear the voice of God

Calling us to respond creatively

And share the gifts we have.

Weston Priory, refrain from "Listen with the Ear of Your Heart," Copyright © 1989 from the recording *Move With One Heart*, The Benedictine Foundation of the State of Vermont, Inc., Weston, Vt. Used by permission.

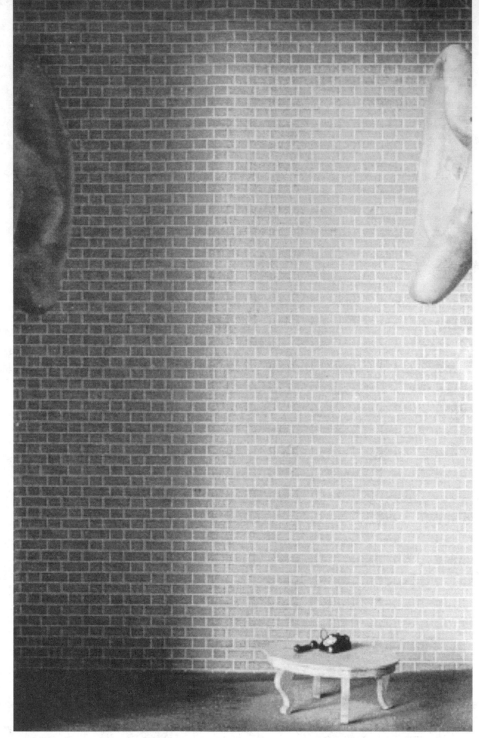

Matthew Inglis, *Walls Have Ears*, 1990, photograph by Ralph Hughes, as reproduced in Bill Hare, *Contemporary Painting in Scotland* (East Roseville, New South Wales, Australia: Craftesmen House, 1990). Used by permission of Craftesmen House.

Place yourself in this picture.
Where do you stand?
What do you hear?

The Word to Jonah

Paul Kittelson and Olin Calk, *Whale*, steel and window screen, Houston, Texas. Used by permission.

If you were the fish, what would your take on the story be?

The word of God came to Jonah
a second time, saying, "Get up,
go to Nineveh, that great city,
and proclaim to it the message
that I tell you."

Jonah 3:1–2

The Prayer of Jonah
(or: the futility of hatred)

Out of my distress I called you, O Lord,
but you did not answer me.

I refused to preach repentance to the Ninevites,
but you forced me.

When I sailed away in the opposite direction,
you hurled a violent wind at me.
Your monster swallowed me and returned me
    to your path.

Repentance I would not preach in Nineveh,
rather I cursed them, "Forty days more and
    Nineveh shall be
    destroyed."

But you did not listen to me.
You listened to the people of Nineveh as they
    sat in ashes
    covered with sackcloth.

I am angry because you are a gracious and
    merciful God,
slow to anger,
rich in clemency,
loathe to punish.

If you will not destroy Nineveh then give me death.
It is better for me to die than to see my enemy live.

Thomas Reese, in *Peace Prayers from Around the World*
(San Francisco: HarperCollins, 1992), 6–7. Used by permission.

Where is Jonah
in this picture?

Albert Pinkham Ryder, *Jonah*, National Museum of American Art, gift of John Gellatly, Smithsonian Institution, Washington, D.C. (National Museum of American Art, Washington, D.C./Art Resource, N.Y.). Used by permission.

Jonah at a Glance

Yes/No.
Stay/Go.
Repent and Change.

- Now the word of God came to Jonah son of Amittai, saying, "Go at once to Nineveh."
- But Jonah set out to flee to Tarshish.
- But God hurled a great wind upon the sea, and the ship threatened to break up.
- The sailors cast lots, and the lot fell on Jonah.
- So they picked Jonah up and threw him into the sea.
- But God provided a large fish to swallow up Jonah.
- Then Jonah prayed to God from the belly of the fish.
- Then God spoke to the fish, and it spewed Jonah out upon the dry land.
- The word of God came to Jonah a second time.
- So Jonah set out and went to Nineveh, according to the word of God.
- And he cried out, "Forty days more, and Nineveh shall be overthrown!"
- And the people of Nineveh believed God; they proclaimed a fast, and put on sackcloth.
- When God saw what they did, God changed and did not destroy Nineveh.
- But this was very displeasing to Jonah, and he became angry.
- And God said, "Is it right for you to be angry?"
- Then Jonah went out of the city and sat waiting to see what would become of the city.
- God appointed a bush to give shade, then God appointed a worm so it withered.
- Jonah asked that he might die.
- But God said to Jonah, "You are concerned about the bush, should I not be concerned about Nineveh?"

A New Teaching

They were all amazed, and they kept on asking one another, "What is this? A new teaching—with authority! Jesus commands even the unclean spirits, and they obey him."

Mark 1:27

When have you learned something that has made you feel whole or that made you able to leap back into your life again? What authority does the teaching of Jesus have for your life?

Linda Post, *Solstice*, 1991, R. Michelson Galleries, Northampton, Mass.
Used by permission of R. Michelson Galleries.

Edvard Munch, *The Scream*, 1893, Nasjonalgalleriet, Oslo, Norway. Used by permission.

The Scream shows one possible response to authority. Where do you think the authority in this picture lies?

Pray with Authority

Jesus spoke with authority,

power, confidence, and energy.

He prayed with authority, too.

Often when we pray, God,

we do not feel that we are filled

      with authority.

We feel powerless,

self-conscious,

timid.

If you are the source of authority,

perhaps we could experience authority

      when speaking to you.

We know we are not Jesus.

But we would be followers of Jesus,

imitators of his authority,

seekers of his closeness to you.

Help us to pray with authority, God.

Amen.

Authorities in My Life	
People with Authority	Sources of Authority

With Wings like Eagles

God gives power to the faint, and strengthens the powerless. Even youths will faint and be weary, and the young will fall exhausted; but those who wait for God shall renew their strength, they shall mount up with wings like eagles, they shall run and not be weary, they shall walk and not faint.

Isaiah 40:29–31

Cliff Bahnimptewa, *Kwahu (Eagle)*, The Heard Museum, Phoenix, Az. Used by permission.

Eagle dances express a longing for the restoration of the past—a return to a life free of hunger, epidemic disease, and war. They also are expressions of youthful energy and hope. The Israelites whom Isaiah addressed also longed for a restoration of the past and sought renewed energy and hope.

Dance with wings like an eagle.

They That Wait upon God

Words: Isaiah 40:31   Music: Traditional

They that wait up-on God shall re-new their strength, they shall mount up on wings as ea - gles, they shall run and not be wea-ry, they shall walk and not faint. Help us, God, help us, God, on our way.

Wilma Rudolph, 1960. used by permission of AP/Wide World Photos.

Wilma Rudolph was the winner of two gold medals in the 1960 Olympics. This photo captures the exhilaration that comes with physical exercise. Weariness comes as well. Have you ever felt exhilaration and exhaustion at the same time?

They shall *run* and not be weary.

O God,
we are made by the good news of your love
for us and for all.
We thank you for creating us
and giving us all that is necessary for life.
We thank you for your action in Christ
by which our lives are measured,
found wanting, and renewed.
Help us remember your gifts
that we may praise you with lives of joy and service;
through Jesus Christ.
Amen

United Church of Christ Book of Worship (New York: Office for Church Life and Leadership, 1986), 535. Used by permission.

God's transforming power surrounds the world.

Clothed with Joy

As you look at the map of the world, try to identify specific places where there are people or situations in need of God's healing.

You have turned my mourning into dancing; you have taken off my sackcloth and clothed me with joy, so that my soul may praise you and not be silent. O Sovereign my God, I will give thanks to you forever.

Psalm 30:11–12

Where do you see God's transforming power at work in the world today?

How do people in other parts of the world celebrate God's healing power?

PSALM 30

Response: May they that sow in tears reap with shouts of joy.

1. I will extol you, O God, for you
   have drawn me up,
       and did not let my foes rejoice
       over me.

2. O God my God, I cried to you for help,
       and you have healed me.

3. O God, you brought up my soul from Sheol,
       restored me to life from among
       those gone down to the Pit.

4. Sing praises to God, O you God's
   faithful ones,
       and give thanks to God's holy
       name. R

5. For God's anger is but for a moment;
   God's favor is for a lifetime.
       Weeping may linger for the night,
       but joy comes with the morning.

6. As for me, I said in my prosperity,
   "I shall never be moved."

7. By your favor, O God, you had
   established me as a strong mountain;
       you hid your face; I was dismayed.

8. To you, O God, I cried,
       and to you I made supplication: R

9. "What profit is there in my death, if I
   go down to the Pit?
       Will the dust praise you? Will it
       tell of your faithfulness?

10. "Hear, O God, and be gracious to me!
    O God, be my helper!"

11. You have turned my mourning into dancing:
    you have taken off my sackcloth
    and clothed me with joy,

12. so that my soul may praise you and
    not be silent.
        O God, my God, I will give thanks
        to you forever. R

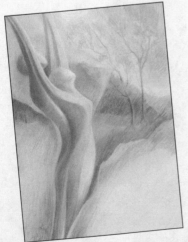

These people seem illuminated by joy.
Their arms are stretched up and out in prayer.
Have you ever prayed while standing this way?

Mary Southard, CSJ, *Created to Praise*, Sisters of St. Joseph,
LaGrange Park, Ill. Used by permission.

I Will Do a New Thing

Do not remember the former things, or consider the things of old. I am about to do a new thing; now it springs forth, do you not perceive it? I will make a way in the wilderness and rivers in the desert.

Isaiah 43:18–19

© Bill Barrett. Used by permission.

First Sight

Most Holy One,
　　We lay before you
　　　　in our minds and hearts
　　　　　　the many situations, ideas
　　　　　　thoughts and deeds
　　　　　　that make us captive.
We are both
　　willing and unwilling captives
　　　　of the powers that
　　　　　　darken and diminish life.
You are both
　　light and the blowing wind
　　　　of liberty.
Make us into freedom-makers.
May it be.

Daniel H. Evans, *Alive Now!*, May/June 1985,
65. Used by permission of the author.

When this photograph was taken, these children were living in a refugee camp in Honduras. They and their families fled El Salvador because of a civil war there. There are very few pictures of older youth in refugee camps like this one because most older youth were fighting each other in the war.

However, these refugees found renewal and new life. In 1990 they decided to leave the refugee camps and went home to El Salvador. They built new homes in a new town that they named after a murdered Jesuit priest, Segundo Montes.

i am about to do a new thing.

God
is doing a new thing.

Who I am
is not
who I was
and not
who I will become.
Which one
is really me?

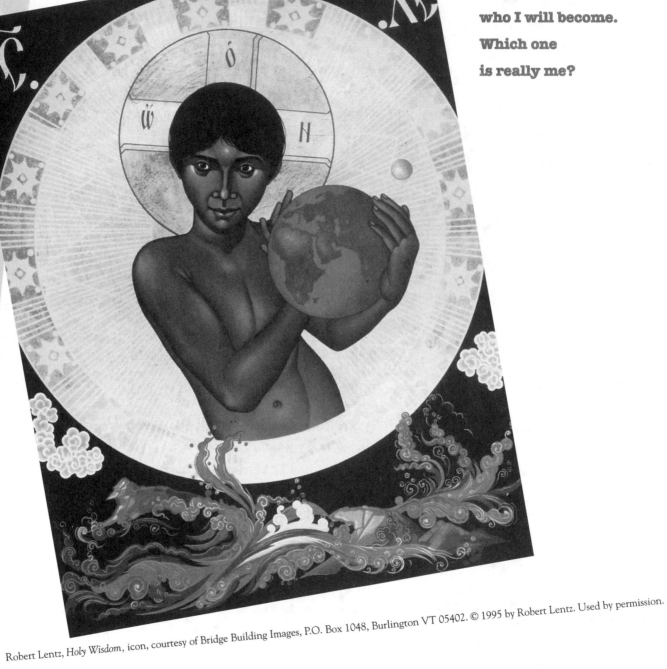

Robert Lentz, *Holy Wisdom*, icon, courtesy of Bridge Building Images, P.O. Box 1048, Burlington VT 05402. © 1995 by Robert Lentz. Used by permission.

God's creating power of wisdom is pictured here as an older youth. God's Holy Wisdom is always available to guide you from your past into your future. Behold, God is doing a new thing!

in Levi's House

As Jesus sat at dinner in Levi's house, many tax collectors and sinners were also sitting with Jesus and the disciples—for there were many who followed him. When the scribes of the Pharisees saw that he was eating with sinners and tax collectors, they said to the disciples, "Why does Jesus eat with tax collectors and sinners?" When Jesus heard this, he said to them, "Those who are well have no need of a physician, but those who are sick; I have come to call not the righteous but sinners."

Mark 2:15–17

John Perceval, *Christ Dining at Young and Jackson's,* 1947, private collection of Helen and Maurice Alther, Melbourne, Australia. Used by permission of the artist.

John Perceval's busy painting shows a large gathering of people. What stories do you find in this painting?

Invisible Barriers

The walls that keep me out cannot be seen
but they are as real
as brick
and mortar.
The walls that keep me out cannot be heard
but they are as real
as words
of hatred.
The walls that keep me out can be torn down
but first you must see
they keep
you in.

Ted Huffman

We Are Your People

Words: Brian Wren, 1973; rev. 1993   Music: John Wilson, 1973

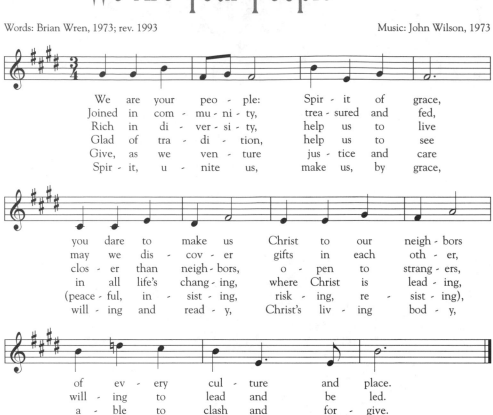

We are your peo - ple: Spir - it of grace,
Joined in com - mu - ni - ty, trea - sured and fed,
Rich in di - ver - si - ty, help us to live
Glad of tra - di - tion, help us to see
Give, as we ven - ture jus - tice and care
Spir - it, u - nite us, make us, by grace,

you dare to make us Christ to our neigh - bors
may we dis - cov - er gifts in each oth - er,
clos - er than neigh - bors, o - pen to strang - ers,
in all life's chang - ing, where Christ is lead - ing,
(peace - ful, in - sist - ing, risk - ing, re - sist - ing),
will - ing and read - y, Christ's liv - ing bod - y,

of ev - ery cul - ture and place.
will - ing to lead and be led.
a - ble to clash and for - give.
where our best ef - forts should be.
wis - dom to know when and where.
lov - ing the whole hu - man race.

Spirit, unite us.

A circle can be a place of closeness and joy. How can the circle be expanded to celebrate the inclusive nature of the church?

UPON A High Mountain

Six days later, Jesus took with him Peter and James and John, and led them up a high mountain apart, by themselves. And he was transfigured before them. Then a cloud overshadowed them, and from the cloud there came a voice, "This is my Child, the Beloved; to this one you shall listen!" Suddenly when they looked around, they saw no one with them any more, but only Jesus.

Mark 9:2, 7–8

Raphael, *The Transfiguration*, detail, Pinacoteca, Vatican Museums, Vatican State, Italy (Scala/Art Resource, N.Y.). Used by permission.

This painting shows more people than are named in Mark 9:2–9.

The two characters at the left seem to be less fearful than the three at the bottom of the page.

Who do you think these characters represent? If you were in this scene, who would you be?

This is my child.

61

In *The Chronicles of Narnia*, C. S. Lewis employs a mythical landscape to explore the world of the spirit.

In this passage, Lucy experiences a kind of transfiguration of understanding.

She begins to realize that the point at which one first fully encounters the Divine will continue to expand one's own spiritual vision.

Lucy stood . . . looking down over the wall of that garden, and seeing all Narnia spread out below. But when you looked down you found that this hill was much higher than you had thought: it sank down . . . thousands of feet below them and trees . . . looked no bigger than grains of green salt. Then she turned . . . and looked at the garden.

"I see," she said at last, thoughtfully. ". . . It is far bigger inside than it was outside."

Of course. . . ." said the Faun. "The further up and the further in you go, the bigger everything gets. The inside is larger than the outside."

Lucy looked hard . . . and saw that it was not really a garden at all but a whole world, with its own rivers and woods and sea and mountains. . . .

"I see," she said. "This is still Narnia, and, more real and more beautiful than the Narnia down below. . . . I see . . . world within world, Narnia within Narnia. . . ."

"Yes," said Mr. Tumnus, "like an onion: except that as you continue to go in and in, each circle is larger than the last."

C. S. Lewis, *The Last Battle*, Book 7 in the *Chronicles of Narnia* (New York: Macmillan, 1956). Used by permission.

What difference does it make in my life that Jesus is God's chosen child?

62

Rainbow Promise

God said, "I establish my covenant with you, that never again shall all flesh be cut off by the waters of a flood, and never again shall there be a flood to destroy the earth." God said, "This is the sign of the covenant that I make between me and you and every living creature that is with you, for all future generations: I have set my bow in the clouds, and it shall be a sign of the covenant between me and the earth."

Genesis 9:11–13

Barbara Reid, With hoot and squawk and squeak and bark . . . The animals tumbled off the ark, in Two by Two (New York: Scholastic, 1992), 27. © 1992 Barbara Reid. All rights reserved. Used by permission of Scholastica Canada, Ltd.

How many kinds of animals can you count?

Do you get the impression that the animals are moving slowly or quickly?

What do you think God's promise means to them?

Noah's Prayer

Lord,
what a menagerie!
Between Your downpour and these
    animal cries
one cannot hear oneself think!
The days are long,
Lord.
All this water makes my heart sink.
When will the ground cease to rock
    under my feet?
The days are long.
Master Raven has not come back.
Here is Your dove.
Will she find us a twig of hope?
The days are long,
Lord.
Guide Your Ark to safety,
some zenith of rest,
where we can escape at last
from this brute slavery.
The days are long,
Lord.
Lead me until I reach the shore of
    Your covenant.

Amen

Carmen Bernos De Gasztold, in *Prayers from the Ark,* trans. Rumer Godden (New York: The Viking Press, 1962), 13. Used by permission of Viking Penguin, a division of Penguin Books USA, Inc.

God's Covenant, in *Vienna Genesis*, Cod. Theol. Graec 31, page 5, Austrian National Library, Vienna, Austria. Used by permission.

God of the Sparrow God of the Whale

Words: Jaroslav J. Vajda, 1983

Tune: ROEDER 5.4.6.7.7.
Carl F. Schalk, 1983

Look at the expressions and postures of the people in this art.

What do you think is going through their minds?

1 God of the spar-row God of the whale
2 God of the earth-quake God of the storm
3 God of the rain-bow God of the cross
4 God of the hun-gry God of the sick
5 God of the neigh-bor God of the foe
6 God of the a-ges God near at hand

God of the swirl-ing stars How does the crea-ture say
God of the trum-pet blast How does the crea-ture cry
God of the emp-ty grave How does the crea-ture say
God of the prod-i-gal How does the crea-ture say
God of the prun-ing hook How does the crea-ture say
God of the lov-ing heart How do your chil-dren say

1–5 | 6

Awe How does the crea-ture say Praise
Woe How does the crea-ture cry Save
Grace How does the crea-ture say Thanks
Care How does the crea-ture say Life
Love How does the crea-ture say Peace
Joy How do your chil-dren say Home.

HOW HOW does the creature say Grace?
does the creature say Thanks?

An Everlasting Covenant

I will make you exceedingly fruitful; and I will make nations of you, and rulers shall come from you. I will establish my covenant between me and you, and your offspring after you throughout their generations, for an everlasting covenant, to be God to you and to your offspring after you.

Genesis 17:6–7

The promises these two sisters made to each other in the book and film *The Color Purple* lasted despite their separation of forty years and thousands of miles. What promises have you made to others? What promises have others made to you?

Prayer for Illumination

O God, you have made promises to all generations. You promised an "everlasting covenant" to Abraham and Sarah, and to all their succeeding generations. Remind us of all the ways you move in our midst, and lead us to give thanks for the promises fulfilled in our lives. We have so many blessings, but we so often forget to notice them and to give thanks for them. Keep us alert and attentive, that we might always notice the promises you keep in our lives. Amen.

Film still from *The Color Purple,*
© 1985, Warner Brothers, Inc.
Photo provided by Photofest,
New York, N.Y. Used by permission.

Nothing Can Trouble

Words and music: The Taizé Community, 1991

♩ = 72

Am   Dm7   G   CM7   F   Bdim/D

Na - da te tur - be, na - da te es - pan - te. Quien a Dios tie - ne
Noth - ing can trou - ble, noth - ing can fright - en. Those who seek God shall

Esus4 E Am   F   Bdim/D   E   Am

na - da le fal - ta.   So - lo Dios bas - ta.
nev - er go want - ing.   God a - lone fills us.

Nothing can trouble us,

for God has given us an everlasting covenant.

Illuminated manuscript, *Abraham Holding in His Lap His Descendants: Jews, Christians, and Muslims,* Bible de Souvigny, Ms 1, f.256, Bibliotheque Municipale, Moulins, France (Giraudon/Art Resource, N.Y.). Used by permission.

This illustration shows Abraham with some of his many descendants. Abraham did not have them alone! In the blank box, draw Sarah and some of her descendants. As a person of faith, you could draw yourself in the box. You are a spiritual descendant of Abraham and Sarah. God's promise to them is kept through you.

Overturn the Tables

In the temple Jesus found people selling cattle, sheep, and doves, and the money changers seated at their tables. He poured out the coins of the money changers and overturned their tables. Jesus told those who sold the doves, "Take these things out of here! Stop making God's house a marketplace!"

John 2:14, 15b–16

Baseball or God?

Hank Greenberg was one of baseball's greatest players, a Jew who played for the Detroit Tigers during the 1930s and 1940s. In the fall of 1934, as his Tigers challenged the mighty New York Yankees for the American League pennant, he was confronted with a sobering decision. On September 19, a day on which the Tigers were to play the Yankees in a very important game, one that would help settle the league championship, Greenberg went not to the ballpark, but to a nearby synagogue for Yom Kippur services. Rather than play in this game of great import, he decided instead to worship God. In order to do what God desired, he decided that he needed to rest and refrain from working (see Leviticus 16:29–34). Even baseball could not supplant God for him.

Based on *Sports Illustrated*, 12 September 1994, 17–18.

El Greco, *Cleansing the Temple*, 1584–94, National Gallery, London, England. Used by permission.

Look at the expressions on the faces in the painting. What do you think Jesus is thinking? How do the people around him appear to be reacting? Does anything in this scene surprise you?

Love *God* and **live** righteously.

El Greco, *Cleansing the Temple*, detail,
1584–94, National Gallery, London, England.
Used by permission.

O God, how easy we find it to place other gods before you. Without even trying, we so often forget that you are first. We put our hope in possessions. We look to buying and selling as the meaning of our lives. We focus on commerce and profit-making as though that is where salvation lies. Turn us toward you, O God, that we might put our trust in you and follow you in everything we do, not just for your sake, but for our own.

Amen.

God so Loved

For God so loved the world that God gave God's only Child, so that everyone who believes in that Child should not perish but have eternal life.

John 3:16

The best way to know God is to love many things.

Vincent van Gogh

My Bath

My bath is the ocean
and I am a continent
with hills and valleys
and earthquakes and storms.
I put the two mountain
       peaks of my knees
under water and bring
       them up again.

Our earth was like that—
great churnings and splashings,
and continents appearing
       and disappearing.

Only you, O God, know about
       it all,
and understand, and take care
of all creation.

Madeleine L'Engle, "My Bath," in *Everyday Prayers* (Ridgefield, CT: Morehouse-Barlow). Copyright © 1974 by Crosswicks, Ltd. Used by permission of Lescher and Lescher.

God's love isn't just for humans, but for the whole world, all of creation.

Richard Bullard, *Satellite Image of Earth*, Tony Stone Images, Chicago, Ill. Used by permission.

Identify as many Christian symbols as you can. How does this stained glass reveal the love of God to you?

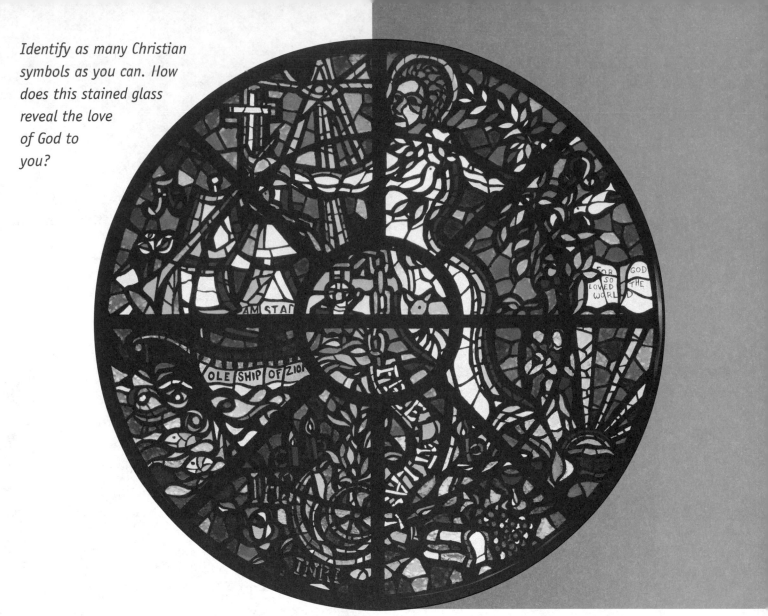

Text visible within the stained glass: FOR GOD SO LOVED THE WORLD; AM STAR; OLE SHIP OF ZION; INRI

David Driskell, *West Window*, 1990, People's Congregational United Church of Christ, Washington, D.C. Used by permission.

L♦VE in word and deed

LOVE

In the Christian sense, love is not primarily an emotion but an act of the will. When Jesus tells us to love our neighbors, he is not telling us to love them in the sense of responding to them with a cozy emotional feeling. You can as well produce a cozy emotional feeling on demand as you can a yawn or a sneeze. On the contrary, he is telling us to love our neighbors in the sense of being willing to work for their well-being even if it means sacrificing our own well-being to that end. . . . Thus in Jesus' terms we can love our neighbors without necessarily liking them. . . .

This does not mean that liking may not be a part of loving, only that it doesn't have to be. Sometimes liking follows on the heels of loving. It is hard to work for somebody's well-being very long without coming in the end to rather like him too.

Frederick Buechner, *Wishful Thinking: A Theological ABC* (New York: Harper and Row, 1973), 54.
Copyright © 1973 by Frederick Buechner. Used by permission of HarperCollins Publishers, Inc.

The Law Within

Charles White, *The Prophet #1*, Heritage Gallery, Los Angeles, Calif. Used by permission.

Look at the prophet's blissful expression and relaxed posture.
What might he be saying to God?

I will put my law within them, and I will write it on their hearts; and I will be their God, and they shall be my people.

Jeremiah 31:33b

O God, we do not always remember you. We do not always live with you at the center. Be with us today, that we might be reminded that all that we have and are comes from you. You have kept us alive and sustained us and allowed us to reach this moment. Thank you. Open us now to you. Amen.

You shall be my people.

Marc Chagall, *Klageleid des Jeremias*, 1956, © ARS,
New York, N.Y. Used by permission.

Look

at the way this man

is holding the Torah, God's law.

How do you think he feels about it?

How do you feel about it?

O God, we look forward to the day when your
covenant will be written on our hearts. But right
now we know that we need all the reminders we
can have that you are sovereign and that our lives
are best when we serve you. Thank you for the
opportunity we have had today to remember your
grace and our response. Go with us as we seek
you in all we do and are. Amen.

*With all my heart, God,
I want to say
to you . . .*

I will write the law on your heart.

jerusalem

Betty LaDuke, *Guatemala: Procession,* Ashland, Oregon. Used by permission.

Then those who went ahead and those who followed were shouting, "Hosanna! Blessed is the one who comes in the name of God! Blessed is the coming dominion of our ancestor David! Hosanna in the highest heaven!" Then Jesus entered Jerusalem and went into the temple.

Mark 11:9–11a

■ **Imagine who the characters in the painting are, and describe their lives.**

■ **Pick a character or shape in the painting.**

What are the eyes of your character telling you about him, her, or it?

Describe the moods and feelings that the eyes convey.

My Commitment to Make a Difference

Jerusalem: the place of desertion and death

73

Max Beckmann, *Landscape, Cannes*, 1934, gift of Louise S. Ackerman, San Francisco Museum of Modern Art, San Francisco, Calif. Used by permission.

Where does this road take you?

Imagine this road as the journey of your faith, both past and future.

Where is it heading?

What have been some of its bright spots?

What have been its shadows?

Where is God in the painting?

Where is this road leading you?

Collect for Palm Sunday

Jesus, when you rode into Jerusalem
the people waved palms
with shouts of acclamation.
Grant that when the shouting dies
we may still walk beside you even to a cross....

A New Zealand Prayer Book: Ite Karakia Mihinare O Aotearoa
(Auckland, New Zealand: William Collins Publishers, 1989),
580–81. Used by permission.

**O Sovereign God, we have seen your love
in the face of Christ; we have heard it in
human words and experienced it in deeds
of kindness and compassion. It is painful
to remember the suffering of Jesus. Help us
to learn from the stories of his last hours
and to find strength for our own journeys
through life. Let your face shine on your
servants, and save us in your steadfast love.
Amen.**

Lavon Bayler, *Fresh Winds of the Spirit: Liturgical
Resources for Year A* (New York: The Pilgrim
Press, 1986), 52. Used by permission.

The journey of faith: not always easy.

Jesus Is risen!

As they entered the tomb, they saw a youth, dressed in a white robe, sitting on the right side; and they were alarmed. But the youth said to them, "Do not be alarmed; you are looking for Jesus of Nazareth, who was crucified. Jesus has been raised, and the body is not here. Look, there is the place they laid the body."

Mark 16:5–6

José Clemente Orozco, *The White House*, 1925–27, Instituto Nacional de Bellas Artes y Literatura, Mexico City, Mexico. Reproduccion autorizada por el instituto Nacional de Bellas Artes y Literatura. Used by permission.

Gaze at the shapes: the brilliant light around the doorway, the shadowy tree, the phantom figures standing at the doorway with hollow eyes. Place yourself in the painting.

What has happened that has left you looking like this?

What are you thinking and feeling at this moment?

What do you imagine happens next?

God of terror and joy, you arise to shake the earth. Open our graves and give us back the past; so that all that has been buried may be freed and forgiven, and our lives may return to you through the risen Christ, Amen.

Janet Morley, *All Desires Known: Prayers Uniting Faith and Feminism* (Wilton, Conn.: Morehouse-Barlow, 1988), 16. Used by permission.

Christ is risen
Christ is risen indeed!

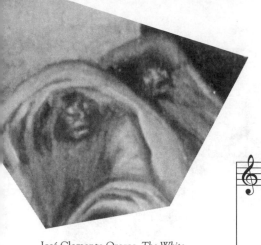

José Clemente Orozco, *The White House*, detail, 1925–27, Instituto Nacional de Bellas Artes y Literatura, Mexico City, Mexico. Reproduccion autorizada por el instituto Nacional de Bellas Artes y Literatura. Used by permission.

God of all loving, you bury our past in the heart of Christ and are going to take care of our future. Amen.

Brother Roger of Taizé, © Ateliers et Presses de Taizé, 71250 Taizé Communauté, France. Used by permission.

Words and music: South African

Refrain

Ha - le - lu - ya! Pe - lo tsa ro - na, di tha - bi - le ka - o - fe - la.
Hal - le - lu - ya! We sing your prais - es, all our hearts with glad - ness are filled.

Ha - le - lu - ya! Pe - lo tsa ro - na, di tha - bi - le ka - o - fe - la.
Hal - le - lu - ya! We sing your prais - es, all our hearts with glad - ness are filled.

Last time, end **Stanzas**

1 Ke Mo - re - na Je - so, ya re du - me - let - seng,
1 Je - sus Christ said to us: I am wine, I am bread,
2 Christ now sends us all out, strong in faith, free of doubt;

To Refrain

ya re du - me - let - seng, ho tsa - mai - sa e - van - ge - di.
I am wine, I am bread, give to all who hun - ger and thirst.
strong in faith, free of doubt; tell to all the joy - ful Good News.

Respond to the risen Christ:
celebrate and love!

Of One Heart and Soul

Faith Ringgold, *Church Picnic*, painted story quilt, Englewood, New Jersey.
Photo by Gamma I. Used by permission.

In what ways is each person sharing at this church picnic? What would it be like to share all you have with others?

Now the whole group of those who believed were of one heart and soul, and no one claimed private ownership of any possessions, but everything they owned was held in common. With great power the apostles gave their testimony to the resurrection of the Sovereign Jesus, and great grace was upon them all.

Acts 4:32–33

The important thing to notice is that "there was not a needy person among them" (v. 34). By seeing to it that the needy are cared for, the early church came to embody the Old Testament ideal (cf. Deut. 15:4). Yet by sharing their goods in common, they also came to embody the Greek ideal, which held that "for friends all things are common." Clearly, Luke is presenting the early church as the embodiment of both the Jewish and Greek ideal community in which unity and charity thrive.

Fred Craddock, *Preaching Through the Christian Year, Year B: A Comprehensive Commentary on the Lectionary*, ed. Fred Craddock, John H. Hayes, Carl R. Holladay, Gene M. Tucker (Valley Forge, Pa.: Trinity Press International, 1993), 238.

Gracious God, we are all too aware of the times we are selfish and unwilling to share. Remind us of the special wonders to which you have treated us in our lives. As you fill us to the brim with a sense of how blessed we are, help us to overflow with kindness and love for others. In the name of the risen Christ, around whom we are gathered as an Easter community, **amen.**

Not a needy person among them.

How I Spend My Time

Great grace was upon them all.

Love

The unabashed *eros* of lovers, the sympathetic *philia* of friends, *agape* giving itself away freely no less for the murderer than for his victim (the King James version translates it as *charity*)—these are all varied manifestations of a single reality. To lose yourself in another's arms, or in another's company, or in suffering for all men who suffer, including the ones who inflict suffering upon you—to lose yourself in such ways is to find yourself. Is what it's all about. Is what love is.

Frederick Buechner, *Wishful Thinking: A Theological ABC* (New York: Harper and Row, Publishers, 1973), 53.

You Are Witnesses

Frederick Horsman Varley, *Liberation*, 1936, gift of John B. Ridley, donated by the Ontario Heritage Foundation, Art Gallery of Ontario, Toronto, Canada. Used by permission of the F. H. Varley Estate/ Mrs. Donald McKay.

What about this painting is reassuring or disturbing? In what ways is the powerful presence of Christ conveyed? If you were one of Jesus' disciples and this risen Christ appeared to you, how might you respond?

Then Jesus opened their minds to understand the scriptures, and said to them, "Thus it is written, that the Messiah is to suffer and to rise from the dead on the third day, and that repentance and forgiveness of sins is to be proclaimed in the Messiah's name to all nations, beginning from Jerusalem. You are witnesses of these things."

Luke 24:45–48

You are witnesses of these things.

Statement of Faith in the Form of a Doxology

We believe in you, O God, Eternal Spirit,
God of our Savior Jesus Christ and our God,
and to your deeds we testify:

> You call the worlds into being,
> create persons in your own image,
> and set before each one the ways of life and death.

> You seek in holy love to save all people from
> aimlessness and sin.

> You judge people and nations by your righteous
> will declared through prophets and apostles.

> In Jesus Christ, the man of Nazareth, our crucified
> and risen Savior,
> you have come to us
> and shared our common lot,
> conquering sin and death
> and reconciling the world to yourself.

> You bestow upon us your Holy Spirit,
> creating and renewing the church of Jesus
> Christ,
> binding in covenant faithful people of all ages,
> tongues, and races.

> You call us into your church
> to accept the cost and joy of discipleship,
> to be your servants in the service of others,
> to proclaim the gospel to all the world
> and resist the powers of evil,
> to share in Christ's baptism and eat at his table,
> to join him in his passion and victory.

> You promise to all who trust you
> forgiveness of sins and fullness of grace,
> courage in the struggle for justice and peace,
> your presence in trial and rejoicing,
> and eternal life in your realm which has no end.

Blessing and honor, glory and power be unto you.
Amen.

United Church of Christ Book of Worship (New York: Office for Church Life and Leadership, 1986), 514. © 1981 United Church of Christ. Used by permission.

ORisen Christ, we are grateful that you walk among us on earth, bringing life and hope. Help us to recognize you; help us to be aware of your presence in our time of worship. Enable us to stand alongside you in your ministry of healing on the crowded roads of our world through the gift of the Holy Spirit. Amen.

Ruth C. Duck, in *Bread for the Journey: Resources for Worship* (New York: The Pilgrim Press, 1981), 47. Used by permission.

Haleluya! Pelo tsa rona
Halleluya! We Sing Your Praises

Words and music: South African

Refrain

Ha - le - lu - ya! Pe - lo tsa ro - na, di tha - bi - le ka - o - fe -
Hal - le - lu - ya! We sing your prais - es, all our hearts with glad - ness are

la. Ha - le - lu - ya! Pe - lo tsa ro - na, di tha - bi - le ka - o - fe -
filled. Hal - le - lu - ya! We sing your prais - es, all our hearts with glad - ness are

Last time, end Stanzas

la. 1 Ke Mo - re - na Je - so, ya re du - me - let - seng,
filled. 1 Je - sus Christ said to us: I am wine, I am bread,
2 Christ now sends us all out, strong in faith, free of doubt;

To Refrain

ya re du - me - let - seng, ho tsa - mai - sa e - van - ge - di.
I am wine, I am bread, give to all who hun - ger and thirst.
strong in faith, free of doubt; tell to all the joy - ful Good News.

Copyright © Walton Music Corporation. Used by permission.

As you look at the picture, what do you see happening? In what sort of witnessing are the faces engaged? What are some ways that you could take Jesus up on this invitation to witness in your daily life?

Osmond Watson, *Hallelujah*, 1969, The National Gallery of Jamaica, Kingston, Jamaica. Photo by Donnette Zacca. Used by permission.

Let Us Love

We know love by this, that Jesus laid down life for us—and we ought to lay down our lives for one another. How does God's love abide in anyone who has the world's goods and sees a brother or sister in need and yet refuses help? Little children, let us love, not in word or speech, but in truth and action.

1 John 3:16–18

Archbishop Oscar Arnulfo Romero became a champion of the poor and a "voice for the voiceless" after attending the funeral mass of an old friend, Rutilio Grande. Grande worked with poor sugar cane workers and supported those who were striking against the plantation owners. Grande, an old man, and a young boy were assassinated. After seeing their bodies and hearing the pain of the *campesinos* (peasants), Romero began speaking out against violence and human rights violations. On March 24, 1980, Archbishop Romero was also assassinated as he celebrated a memorial mass.

Archbishop Oscar Romero, © Octavio Durán, San Antonio, Texas. Used by permission.

Nada te Turbe
Nothing Can Trouble

Words and music: The Taizé Community, 1991

♩ = 72

Am Dm7 G *cresc.* CM7 F Bdim/D

Na - da te tur - be, na - da te es - pan - te. Quien a Dios tie - ne
Noth - ing can trou - ble, noth - ing can fright - en. Those who seek God shall

Esus4 E Am F Bdim/D E Am

na - da le fal - ta. So - lo Dios bas - ta.
nev - er go want - ing. God a - lone fills us.

How did Oscar Romero express love?

Jennifer Jean Casolo, who worked in El Salvador as a Christian educator, was arrested on November 26, 1989, and falsely accused of harboring weapons for leftist rebels. She was kept in Salvadoran police custody for 17 days before being released. This is her story:

"The lieutenant brought in two other interrogators. They fired questions and accusations at me, always the same, accusing me of hiding the weapons, trying to get names. I was frightened. . . . But I felt strong in what I knew was the truth, and I just had to communicate that. . . .

"Maybe an hour into the interrogation, the . . . cries from . . . next door became unbearable. . . . I crossed my legs and closed my eyes, and I said what I say every time I need strength. The words are part of the vows of a Salvadoran . . . woman who was killed in a massacre in 1981. She left her religious order and took vows to the poor. In those vows she said, '[In] a society that lives [for] power, pleasure, and possession, I want to be a sign of what it truly means to love.' I [cried] and said that over and over to give me strength, and to give strength to whoever was crying, moaning, screaming, being hit.

"Then I looked up at my interrogators and said, 'I thought you didn't do this to people.' Because . . . every time I had questioned the cries and

Michael Tracy, *Cruz: La Pasión (Cross: The Passion)*, as reproduced in *The River Pierce: Sacrifice II, 13.4.90* (San Ygnacio/Houston, Texas: The River Pierce Foundation and Rice University Press, 1992), 63. Photograph © Keith Carter. Used by permission.

On Good Friday 1990, Michael Tracy burned his ten-foot-high processional cross in the Rio Grande to honor the sacrifices of persecuted people and the exploited earth.

the moans, they had told me that they didn't mistreat people.

". . . I looked the lieutenant straight in the face, and I repeated those vows. I said, 'I want you to know what I am saying,' and I [continued to cry].

"The lieutenant motioned to the others to go and tell whoever was beating up the man . . . to stop. You see, they know how to stop the evil when they have the will to do it."

Further, Jennifer reflects about her response when the lieutenant asked her why she wanted to suffer: "To tell you the truth, knowing what the Salvadorans were going through in those interrogation booths, seeing them crouched on the floor, day and night, waiting to be interrogated, barefoot and in ragged clothes, I hadn't really thought of myself as suffering. When he said that, I [imagined] Christ on the cross. For one moment I understood the hope of the Salvadorans.

". . . At that moment I understood that my life wasn't mine. I had given it over as all Salvadorans who struggle for a better life for their children choose to do.

"You don't just face death. You give your life over to the oneness with God, and to the oneness with your brothers and sisters. That's what comes out of the suffering.

"And I said to him, 'You know, suffering isn't the worst thing. Being cruel is a lot worse.' "

Jennifer Jean Casolo, "The Third Interrogation: The Power of Truth in a Salvadoran Prison," *Sojourners* 19, no. 3 (April 1990), 15. Reprinted by permission of *Soujourners*, 2401 15th St. NW, Washington, D.C. 20009; 202-328-8842 / fax 202-328-8757.

 "You don't just face death.
You give your life over to the oneness with God,
and to the oneness with your brothers and sisters."

Jennifer Jean Casolo

ABIDE IN ME

Abide in me as I abide in you.
Just as the branch cannot bear
fruit by itself unless it abides in
the vine, neither can you unless
you abide in me. I am the vine,
you are the branches. Those
who abide in me and I in them
bear much fruit, because apart
from me you can do nothing.

John 15:4–5

**Put yourself in the picture.
If you were a branch on Jesus'
vine, where would you be?
What would it be like to be
part of this tree of life?**

Robert Lentz, *Tree of Life*,
Bridge Building Images,
Burlington, Vt.
Used by permission.

It is crucial that we be rooted
in someone, if not somewhere.
Pilgrim people on the move
root in relationships.
I am the vine, said Jesus,
extending himself through time and space
to graft us as branch.
To claim that continuity
we must submit ourselves to pruning,
sinking ourselves unconditionally
into the will of him in whom
we live and move and are.

Miriam Therese Winter, "Roots," in *God-with-Us: Resources
for Prayer and Praise* (Nashville: Abingdon, 1979), 84.
Copyright Medical Mission Sisters, Philadelphia PA 19111.
Used by permission.

Those who abide in me and

I in them bear much fruit, because
apart from me you can do nothing.

John 15:5

So through you who are life

we will produce the fruit of life

if we choose to engraft ourselves into you.

Catherine of Siena, "Prayer 17," in *The Prayers of Catherine of Siena*, ed. Suzanne Noffke (New York: Paulist Press, 1983), lines 86–88, p. 149. Used by permission.

Photograph by Bill Barrett. Used by permission.

In Madeleine L'Engle's story *A Wind in the Door*, farandolae are creatures who are born to "deepen" and become rooted. The evil Echthroi tempt Sporos, one of the farandolae and the offspring of Senex, to avoid the deepening process. Sporos speaks:

"Farandolae are born to Deepen."

"Fool. Once you Deepen and put down roots you won't be able to romp around as you do now."

"But—"

"You'll be stuck in one place forever with those fuddy-duddy farae, and you won't be able to run or move, ever again."

"But—"

The strength and calm of Senex cut through the ugliness. "It is only when we are fully rooted that we are really able to move."

Indecision quivered throughout Sporos.

Senex continued, "It is true, small offspring. Now that I am rooted I am no longer limited by motion. Now I may move anywhere in the universe. I sing with the stars. I dance with the galaxies. I share in the joy—and in the grief. We farae must have our part in the rhythm of the mitochondria, or we cannot be. If we cannot be, then we are not."

Madeleine L'Engle, *A Wind in the Door* (New York: Farrar, Straus and Giroux, 1973), 190. Copyright © 1973 by Crosswick, Ltd. Used by permission of Farrar, Straus & Giroux, Inc.

Sing a New Song

O sing to God a new song. God has remembered God's steadfast love and faithfulness to the house of Israel. All the ends of the earth have seen the victory of our God.

Psalm 98:1a, 3

Ma Rainey: The blues help you get out of bed in the morning. You get up knowing you ain't alone. There's something else in the world. Something's been added by that song. This be an empty world without the blues. I take that emptiness and try to fill it up with something.

Toledo: You fill it up with something the people can't be without, Ma. That's why they call you the Mother of the Blues. You fill up that emptiness in a way ain't nobody ever thought of doing before. And now they can't be without it.

Ma Rainey: I ain't started the blues way of singing. The blues always been there.

Cutler: In the church sometimes you find that way of singing. They got blues in the church.

Ma Rainey: They say I started it . . . but I didn't. I just helped it out. Filled up that empty space a little bit. That's all.

August Wilson, *Ma Rainey's Black Bottom* (New York: New American Library, 1985), 83. Used by permission.

James Chapin, *Ruby Green Sings*, Norton Gallery of Art, West Palm Beach, Fla. Used by permission of the James Chapin Estate.

The blues, an African American form of music, has musical origins in black gospel church music. It employs poetry, harmony, and improvisation in creating music from the struggles and victories of everyday life and its work, love, and suffering.

Even nature sings praises to God...

After the [leader's] death, his disciples came together and talked about the things he had done. When it was Rabbi Schneur Zalman's turn, he asked them: "Do you know why our master went to the pond every day at dawn and stayed there for a little while before coming home again?" They did not know why. Rabbi Zalman continued: "He was learning the song with which the frogs praise God. It takes a very long time to learn that song."

Martin Buber, *Tales of the Hasidim: The Masters*, trans. Olga Perlzweig (New York: Random House, 1947). Used by permission.

The Doxology
(A song of praise to God)

Praise God, from whom all blessings flow;
Praise God, all creatures here below;
Praise God above, ye heavenly hosts;
Creator, Christ, and Holy Ghost. Amen.

People sing new songs in many ways.
What other ways of singing new songs
could you add to this picture?

THAT THEY MayBe One

Jesus said, "I am no longer in the world, but they are in the world, and I am coming to you. Holy God, Father and Mother, protect them in your name that you have given me, so that they may be one, as we are one."

John 17:11

Lord Christ,
at times we are like strangers on this earth,
disconcerted by all the violence and harsh oppositions.
Like a gentle breeze,
You breathe upon us the Spirit of peace.
Transfigure the deserts of our doubts
and so prepare us to be bearers of reconciliation
wherever you place us,
until a hope of peace arises in our world.

Taizé, "Prayers by Brother Roger," *Praying Together in Word and Song*, rev. ed. (Oxford: A. R. Mowbray & Co. Ltd., 1985), 23. Used by permission.

That All May Be One, United Church of Christ Headquarters, Cleveland, Ohio. Used by permission.

The cross, the circle, the people holding hands, and the sign "All may be one" evoke the hope for unity through Christ among Christians all over the world.

MOVE INTO THE WORLD WITH A HEART AT REST.

Jesus prayed for the disciples "that they may be one, as we are one." Henri J. M. Nouwen points to the same kind of unity as he speaks of the profound unity between prayer and the call to minister to people and society: "The great emphasis on prayer in ministry is not meant as an incentive to be less involved with people or to leave untouched our society with its many struggles. . . . The prayer of the heart is indeed the way to the purity of heart that gives us eyes to see the reality of our existence. This purity of heart allows us to see more clearly, not only our own needy, distorted, and anxious self but also the caring face of our compassionate God. When that vision remains clear and sharp, it will be possible to move into the midst of a tumultuous world with a heart at rest. It is this restful heart that will attract those who are groping to find their way through life. When we have found our rest in God we can do nothing other than minister. God's rest will be visible wherever we go and whoever we meet. And before we speak any words, the Spirit of God, praying in us, will make his presence known and gather people into a new body, the body of Christ."

Henri J. M. Nouwen, *The Way of the Heart: Desert Spirituality and Contemporary Ministry* (New York: The Seabury Press, 1981), 89–90. Used by permission.

Ellen Weiss Falkner, Cleveland Heights, Ohio. Used by permission.

Where are Christians working together to build God's dominion?

Where are Christians working with people of other faiths to make the world better?

Jesus, Risen Lord,
you change and transfigure our heart
    just as it is.
You do not even ask us to uproot the weeds;
you take care of that.
With our own wounds, the thorns that
    hurt us, you
light a fire—and a way forward opens
    in us to
welcome your Spirit of compassion
    and the Spirit of
praise that brings healing.
So that what is most resistant in us,
    our failures,
our refusals and our inner abysses,
    may be transfigured
into energies of love and reconciliation,
all you ask of us is that we welcome you
and rejoice in the miracle of your forgiveness.

Taizé, "Prayers by Brother Roger," *Praying Together in Word and Song*, rev. ed. (Oxford: A. R. Mowbray & Co. Ltd., 1985), 22. Used by permission

Spirit of Comfort

The Spirit helps us in our weakness; for we do not know how to pray as we ought, but that very Spirit intercedes with sighs too deep for words. And God, who searches the heart, knows what is the mind of the Spirit, because the Spirit intercedes for the saints according to the will of God.

Romans 8:26–27

**Come down, O Love divine,
Seek out this soul of mine
And visit it with Your own ardor glowing;
O Comforter, draw near, Within my heart appear,
And kindle it, Your holy flame bestowing.**

Bianco da Siena, "Come Down, O Love Divine," trans. Richard Frederick Littledale, in *The Presbyterian Hymnal* (Louisville: Westminster/John Knox Press, 1990), 313. Used by permission.

A variety of persons find comfort and warmth in the fire burning in the can. The image of fire is used to describe the coming of the Spirit on the day of Pentecost in Acts 2:3: *Divided tongues, as of fire, appeared among them, and a tongue rested on each of them.*

Beauford Delaney, *Can Fire in the Park*, 1946, National Museum of American Art, Washington, D.C. (National Museum of American Art, Washington, D.C./Art Resource, N.Y.). Used by permission.

Comfort

com = with

fort = strong

The word *comfort* comes from roots that suggest "to be strong with."

A Litany for Pentecost

When the day of Pentecost had come they were all together in one place and all of the many foreigners heard the witnesses speaking in their own tongue.

Come, Holy Spirit, witness to us also in our several languages.

Speak in the language of our need.

Let us hear how our deepest hungers, desires, and aspirations can be fulfilled by your goodness and in your service.

Come, Holy Spirit, give us that good news again.

Speak in the language of our fear.

Let us hear how our worries about the future, and about each other, and about ourselves, can find rest in your providential care.

Come, Holy Spirit, give us that encouraging news again. . . .

Speak in the language of our gratitude.

Let us hear how our honest thanks relate us, not only to those with whom we live, but also to you, the Lord and Giver of life.

Come, Holy Spirit, give us that enlarging news again. . . .

Speak to us in the language of hope.

Let us hear how our yearning and our expectations are not just wishful thinking, but responses to your promise.

Come, Holy Spirit, give us that good news again. . . .

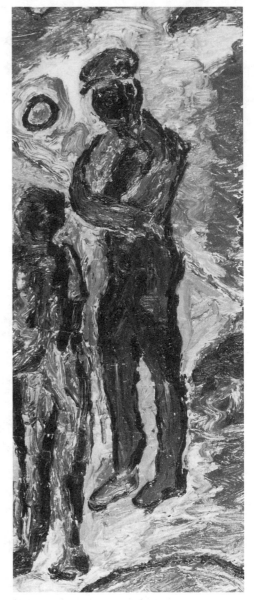

Beauford Delaney, *Can Fire in the Park*, detail, 1946, National Museum of American Art, Washington, D.C. (National Museum of American Art, Washington, D.C./Art Resource, N.Y.). Used by permission.

"A Litany for Pentecost," from *Models for Ministers I,* in *The Wideness of God's Mercy: Litanies to Enlarge Our Prayer,* ed. Jeffrey W. Rowthorn (Minneapolis: The Seabury Press, 1985), 1:126–27. Used by permission.

Come, Holy Spirit.

HOLY, HOLY, HOLY, HOLY

In the year that King Uzziah died, I saw God sitting on a throne, high and lofty; and the hem of God's robe filled the temple. Seraphs were in attendance above God. And one called to another and said: "Holy, holy, holy is the God of hosts; the whole earth is full of God's glory."

Isaiah 6:1–2a, 3

Here is a medieval depiction of Isaiah's vision. The seraphs' posture directs the viewer's attention to God. The outspread arms of God invite the viewer into the painting. How do you imagine the awe-inspiring God?

If we take the . . . vision which the prophet experienced in the temple, we can see that he is saying at least two things which are essential to any understanding of the reality of God: God is far off, unapproachable, mysterious, uncontrollable; and yet, amazingly, this same unapproachable and mysterious God draws us near and touches us. . . . These two, the beyondness and the nearness, are always held together in tension.

Edmund A. Steimle, "God Far— God Near," in *God the Stranger* (Philadelphia: Fortress, 1979), 46. Used by permission of Augsburg Fortress Press.

Manuscript illumination, *The Vision of Isaiah*, c. 1000, Staatsbibliothek, Bamberg, Germany. Used by permission.

AWE-INSPIRING GOD, YOU ARE

Manuscript illumination, *The Vision of Isaiah*, detail, c. 1000, Staatsbibliothek, Bamberg, Germany. Used by permission.

In mystery and grandeur
we see the face of God
in earthiness and the ordinary
we know the love of Christ.

In heights and depths
and life and death:
the spirit of God
is moving among us.

Let us praise God.

I will light a light
in the name of God
who lit the world
and breathed the breath of life into me.

I will light a light
in the name of the Son
who saved the world
and stretched out his hand to me.

I will light a light
in the name of the Spirit
who encompasses the world
and blesses my soul with yearning.

We will light three lights
for the trinity of love:
God above us,
God beside us,
God beneath us:
the beginning,
the end,
the everlasting one.

Michael Shaw and Paul Indwood, "Litany of the Spirit," in *In Spirit and in Truth* (London: St. Thomas More, 1978), 7. Used by permission.

You are a fire, ever burning and never consumed. . . . You are a light, ever shining and never fading. . . . You are goodness beyond all goodness, beauty beyond all beauty, wisdom beyond all wisdom. . . .

Catherine of Sienna, "Sea, Light, Fire," in *The HarperCollins Book of Prayers*, ed. Robert Van de Weyer (San Francisco: HarperSan Francisco, 1993), 89–90. Used by permission.

Manuscript illumination, *The Vision of Isaiah*, detail, c. 1000, Staatsbibliothek, Bamberg, Germany. Used by permission.

On the Sabbath?

One sabbath Jesus was going through the grainfields; and as they made their way the disciples began to pluck heads of grain. The Pharisees said to Jesus, "Look, why are they doing what is not lawful on the sabbath?"

Mark 2:23–24

What do you think the man is doing in this wheat field?

What does the position of his hands suggest to you?

What does the expression on his face convey?

Ben Shahn, *Beatitude*, 1952, private collection. Used by permission of VAGA.

The Cost of a Changing Day

Ever present God:
Everything is in Your hands.
You ordained everything; ordered
everything.
You made all ages a preparation for
the coming of Your Son.
You called your people out of Egypt
to cradle Him.
Your prophets foretold Him, Son
of David, infant of Mary.
Wielding the hammer,
treading the winepress,
tramping the earth,
contradicting the smooth,
giving hope to the sinners,
redeeming the world.

Ever present God
Everything is still in Your hands.
Out of eternity You have called each one of us
into Your Church.
By the spirit of prophecy
You have awakened our souls to expectancy.
By most strange choosing
it is we You have named
to redeem the world by faith in You,
continuing Your incarnation. . . .

Take us O God and remake us.
Give us boldness to enter through the veil
that is His flesh: Knowing in fullness of faith
that our hearts are cleansed from an evil conscience:
so that we may consider one another,
and provoke one another to good works,
and open our minds and hearts
to the meaning and the cost of a changing day.

George F. MacLeod, in *The Whole Earth Shall Cry Glory* (Glasgow: The Iona Community/Wild Goose Publications, 1985), 20–21. Used by permission.

Paul Tillich says, "... new ways of disclosing the world have always aroused the resistance of those who wanted to stay securely with the familiar. . . . It is the fate of every unfamiliar way of looking at the world." Following God's law sometimes means reversing the familiar visions of the world.

Paul Tillich, "Address on the Occasion of the Opening of the New Galleries and Sculpture Garden of the Museum of Modern Art," in *On Art and Architecture*, ed. John Dillenberger and Jane Dillenberger (New York: Crossroad, 1987), 247.

Teach me, O God, the way of your statutes.
Psalm 119:33a

The Eternal

Because we look not at what can be seen but at what cannot be seen; for what can be seen is temporary, but what cannot be seen is eternal. For we know that if the earthly tent we live in is destroyed, we have a building from God, a house not made with hands, eternal in the heavens.

2 Corinthians 4:18–5:1

Christo and Jeanne-Claude, *Running Fence, Sonoma and Marin Counties, California, 1972–1976*, © Christo, 1976, photo by Jeanne-Claude. Used by permission.

The running fence seems to have no beginning and no end. Notice how it seems to continue at the horizon. It gives us an image to help us think about eternity. The dictionary says that which is eternal has no beginning and no end. It exists through all time.

95

Everything we do and are
resides in God's eternal care.

No ray of sunshine is ever lost . . . but the green which it awakens into existence needs time to sprout, and it is not always granted for the sower to see the harvest. All work that is worth anything is done in faith.

Albert Schweitzer

Gracious God, Power of Life, we praise you that you have not abandoned us to the living death of sin and despair, but that, with Jesus Christ, you have lifted us up from the grave. Grant that we might live in newness of life, that we might ourselves know the power of resurrection, now and in the world to come; for it is in the name of the risen Christ that we pray. Amen.

Ruth C. Duck, in *Bread for the Journey: Resources for Worship*, ed. Ruth C. Duck (New York: The Pilgrim Press, 1981), 46. Used by permission.

GOD RELEASE US FROM OUR FEAR.

CHRIST COME CLOSE AND HOLD US NEAR.

WAKE IN US A PURE DESIRE

FOR YOUR KISS, O WIND AND FIRE.

BLOW AGAIN UPON THIS EARTH.

GIVE OUR TREMBLING FLESH REBIRTH.

From "Suddenly God's Sovereign Wind," words by Thomas H. Troeger, copyright; used by permission of Oxford University Press.

Christo and Jeanne-Claude, *Running Fence, Sonoma and Marin Counties, California*, detail, 1972–1976, © Christo, 1976, photo by Jeanne-Claude. Used by permission.

Live by Faith

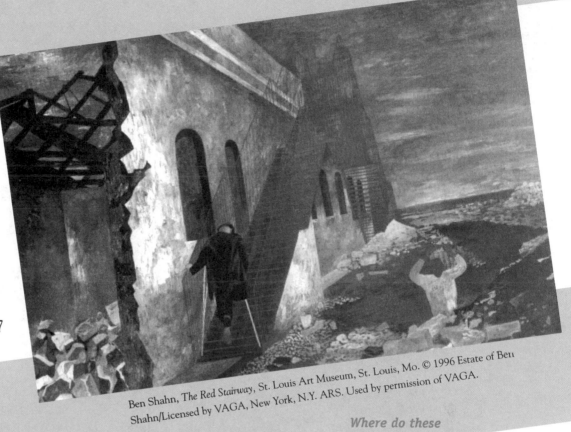

Ben Shahn, *The Red Stairway*, St. Louis Art Museum, St. Louis, Mo. © 1996 Estate of Ben Shahn/Licensed by VAGA, New York, N.Y. ARS. Used by permission of VAGA.

So we
are always
confident;
for we walk
by faith,
not by sight.

2 Corinthians 5:6a, 7

I Believe

I believe that there's

Still hope to live,—not merely to exist,

Somewhere in this

Hopeless whirlpool of life

—a hand extended to help.

In these battered days,

You will find, if you search,

—one who has offered to mend.

I know that somewhere,

In this canyon of despair,

—there's a place of relief.

Somewhere, in this

Turmoil of confusion,

—a right path to follow

Within this world

Of make-believe,

—a faithful friend awaits you.

In this polluted time,

We lead—a hope to be made clean.

Lai Leng Woon, a seventeen-year-old girl from Singapore, quoted in Choan-Seng Song, Third-Eye Theology: Theology in Formation in Asian Settings (Maryknoll, N.Y.: Orbis Books, 1979), 243. Used by permission.

Where do these two people seem to be walking?

How do they seem to be walking?

In what ways might they be walking by faith rather than by sight?

The children seem
to be climbing.
The taller sister
goes before and the
smaller sister follows
her. Think of situations
in your life where
you had confidence
because of someone
who "went before" you.

Ethan Hubbard, *Sisters in the Wind*, as reproduced in Ethan Hubbard, *Straight to the Heart:
Children of the World* (Chelsea, Vt.: Craftsbury
Common Books, 1992). Used by permission of
the photographer.

Psalm 92:12—15

The righteous flourish like the palm tree,

   and grow like a cedar in Lebanon.

They are planted in the house of the Sovereign,

   they flourish in the courts of our God.

They still bring forth fruit in old age,

   they are ever full of sap and green,

to show that God is upright,

   my rock, in whom there is no unrighteousness.

An Inclusive-Language Lectionary: Readings for Year C (New York: The Pilgrim Press, 1985), 70. Used by permission.

David
and Goliath

But David said to the Philistine, "You come to me with sword and spear and javelin; but I come to you in the name of the God of hosts, the God of the armies of Israel, whom you have defied. This very day God will deliver you into my hand."

1 Samuel 17:45–46a

Manuscript illumination, *David and Goliath*, from *León Bible, 1162*, Cod. I,3, pol 131, León Colequta de san Isidoro. Ampliaciones y Reproducciones Mas (Arixu Mas). Used by permission of Arixu Mas.

Do you think God is present in the midst of political struggles? in the midst of war? If so, how? In what ways, if any, might your struggles be compared to an image of battle?

If I could talk to each youngster . . . I would have one message to give them. I would say, "You are important to the world. You are needed. Most of all, you can make a difference in someone else's life. Begin by doing something that shows you care. That's where satisfaction in life begins. And if one day you get a feeling that says you can change the world, trust that feeling. Because *you* make a difference. There is something important that needs to happen in the world because of you, and it *can* happen if you do it."

Mary Conway Kohler, *Young People Learning to Care* (New York: The Seabury Press), 9.

O God of Life, there is much that deals in doubt and despair and death in our world, and we are often tempted to succumb to these forces. Help us always to choose life; to affirm what can be affirmed; to hope where hope is possible; and to risk ourselves to lift up human dignity. For we pray in the name of Christ, who is the way and the truth and the life. Amen.

Ruth C. Duck, in *Bread for the Journey: Resources for Worship*, ed. Ruth C. Duck (New York: The Pilgrim Press, 1981), 63. Used by permission.

Sometimes God does magnificent and powerful work through those who, like David, seem to be vulnerable.

You can make a difference.

Gian Lorenzo Bernini, *David*, 1623, Galleria Borghese, Rome, Italy (Scala/Art Resource, N.Y.). Used by permission.

Jean Ipoustéguy, *David and Goliath*, The Museum of Modern Art, New York, N.Y. Used by permission

litany

Leader: O Holy One, you are our God.

People: We will exalt you, we will praise your name.

Leader: For you have done wonderful things.

People: Plans formed of old, faithful and sure.

Leader: You have been a stronghold to the poor,

People: A stronghold to the needy in distress.

Leader: You subdue the noise of violence and hatred,

People: As the shade of a cloud subdues the heat.

Leader: O Holy One, you are God.

People: We exalt you, we praise your loving name.

Roger Straw, in *Bread for the Journey: Resources for Worship*, ed. Ruth C. Duck (New York: The Pilgrim Press, 1981), 55. Used by permission.

Generous Acts

Clara Hale's generous acts saved children's lives.

Stephen Shames/Matrix, *Mother Clara Hale at Age 87,* as reproduced in *The African Americans* (New York: Penguin Books, 1993). Used by permission of Matrix International, Inc.

For if the eagerness is there, the gift is acceptable according to what one has—not according to what one does not have.

2 Corinthians 8:12

Clara McBride Hale's long career caring for children began when, as a young widow, she had to provide for her own three children. She did so by taking in foster children. After retiring from foster care, a young woman appeared at her door with a drug-addicted baby. Mother Hale then began to take care of addicted children. As the numbers of these children grew, she founded Hale House, a safe, loving environment that has nurtured more than 1,000 young victims of New York City's drug and AIDS epidemics. Before her death at age 87 in 1992, Mother Hale provided a home for children for more than four decades.

"And the one who had little did not have too little."

2 Corinthians 8:15b

God is generous

Stephen Shames/Matrix, *Mother Clara Hale at Age 87*, detail, as reproduced in *The African Americans* (New York: Penguin Books, 1993). Used by permission of Matrix International, Inc.

Most generous God, the gift of Christ is more than we can imagine. Thank you. We also thank you for the lives of all persons who are generous with their gifts. Help us to be as generous with all you have given to us. Amen.

Offertory

Words and music: Ray Makeever, 1984

1 What have we to of-fer? What have we to share?
2 What have we to of-fer? What have we to bring?
3 What have we to of-fer? What have we to give?

Coins____ from the cof-fer, hearts____ filled with care;
Love,____ ripe with laugh-ter; hope, that we can sing;
Eyes that are wide o-pen; lies that we won't live;

God____ will not fal-ter if____ we will dare
dreams of what we're af-ter, prom-is-es of when;
truth that must be spo-ken, jus-tice some-how;

For you know the generous act of Jesus Christ.

2 Corinthians 8:9a

Last time only

lay it at the al-tar there. *(To beginning)*
lay it at the al-tar then. *(To beginning)*
lay it at the al-tar now. *(Continue)* What have we to of-fer?

What have we to give? Lives we will live.

From *With All My Heart: Songs and Liturgies of Encouragement and Hope* (Lima, Ohio: Fairway Press, 1984). Copyright © 1984 by Ray Makeever. Used by permission.

Sent by Jesus

Jesus called the twelve and began to send them out two by two, and gave them authority over the unclean spirits. Jesus ordered them to take nothing for their journey except a staff.

Mark 6:7–8a

Take nothing for your journey except a staff.

Sending the Twelve, Vie de Jesus Mafa, 24 rue du Marechal, Joffre, 28000 Versailles, France. All rights reserved. Used by permission.

A staff had a variety of uses in the Bible. It was used by shepherds to guide a flock of sheep. Travelers often used a staff as a walking stick and to defend themselves against thieves. A staff was also a symbol of prophetic, priestly, or royal authority.

Shin Young-Hun, *Outreach of the New Covenant*, as reproduced in *The Bible Through Asian Eyes*, ed. Masao Takenaka and Ron O'Grady (Auckland, New Zealand: Pace Publishing in association with the Asian Christian Art Association, 1991), 163. Used by permission.

A Prayer of Thanksgiving

Even though we walk through shadowy valleys, God,

we fear no evil. You are with us.

Your rod and your staff comfort us.

Thank you, God, for comfort and strength.

Thank you for your presence.

Thank you for sending us in your name.

Amen.

The work of Jesus is to continue, and for that purpose the church is called and sent. For that work Jesus grants the word and the power that characterized his own ministry. The church is to go trusting this to be true, never contradicting that trust with the excess baggage of security and wealth that offers the world the image of unbelief. There will be rejection and refusal to listen, to be sure, but there will also be those who will welcome both the ministry and the minister.

Fred Craddock, *Preaching Through the Christian Year, Year B: A Comprehensive Commentary on the Lectionary*, ed. Fred B. Craddock, John H. Hayes, Carl R. Holladaya, and Gene M. Tucker (Valley Forge, Pa.: Trinity Press International, 1993), 336.

Thuma Mina

Send Me Now

South African traditional song

How many figures do you see in this painting?

Who do you think they are?

What do they seem to be doing?

DANCE BEFORE GOD

Richmond Barthé, *Exodus Dance*, Harlem River House, New York, N.Y., as reproduced in Cedric Dover, *American Negro Art* (Greenwich, Conn.: New York Graphic Society, 1960), 100. Photograph courtesy of General Services Administration, National Archives and Records, Washington, D.C.

The story of the Exodus is about God's people being freed from slavery in Egypt.

When have you experienced God's freeing power?

Have you ever felt like dancing for joy because of God's actions or presence?

This is what we are here for; to learn to love and enjoy Your Presence and all of the good things of earth as they lead us closer to You.

Robert J. Kreyche, *The Making of a Saint* (Staten Island, N.Y.: Alba House, 1973), 164.

David and all the house of Israel were dancing before God with all their might, with songs and lyres and harps and tambourines and castanets and cymbals.

2 Samuel 6:5

Photo still from *Footloose*, © Paramount Pictures, 1984.
Photo provided by Photofest, New York, N.Y. Used by permission.

"Dancing is celebration!"
His voice carried to the rafters
of the draughty old room.
"It cleans out the body
and the spirit, and energy
that might turn destructive
suddenly becomes an expression
of joy and happiness. For what?
Well, for just about everything."

From the 1984 movie *Footloose*, which tells the story
of a teenage boy, Ren MacCormack, and his struggle
to bring dance back to a sorrowing small town.

Footloose, 1984 in novel form. Published by Wallaby Books
under exclusive license from Paramount Pictures
Corporation, © 1984 by Paramount Pictures Corporation.
Used by permission.

I cannot dance, O Lord,
Unless You lead me.
If You wish me to leap joyfully,
Let me see You dance and sing—

Then I will leap into Love—
And from Love into Knowledge,
And from Knowledge into the Harvest,
That sweetest fruit beyond human sense.

There I will stay with You, whirling.

Mechthild of Magdeburg, "I Cannot Dance," in *Women in Praise of the Sacred*,
ed. Jane Hirshfield (New York: HarperCollins, 1994), 86. Used by permission.

Dance for joy!

InOneBody

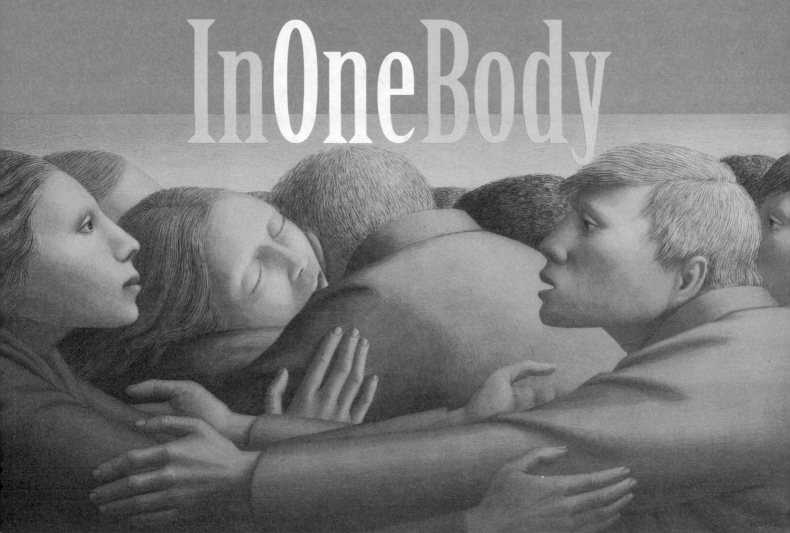

George Tooker, *Embrace of Peace*, 1988, Hartland, Vermont. Used by permission of the artist.

What do you think these people's relationships to one another have been?

What do you think is the story behind this painting?

Christ has abolished the law with its commandments and ordinances, in order to create in Christ one new humanity in place of the two, thus making peace, and in order to reconcile both groups to God in one body through the cross.

Ephesians 2:15–16a

Jesus said: "The wind blows where it pleases. You hear its sound, but you cannot tell where it comes from or where it is going. So it is with everyone (who is) born of the Spirit" (John 3:8).

The Holy Spirit calls us toward an all-inclusive attitude, a theology of the wind, a relationship to God and the world that does not try to make things easy by ruling out whole areas of human experience and whole groups of human beings.

Virginia Ramey Mollenkott, *Godding* (New York: Crossroad, 1987), 38–39.

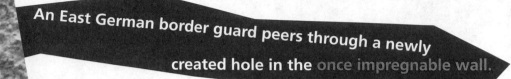

An East German border guard peers through a newly created hole in the once impregnable wall.

For Christ is our peace;
who has made us both one and
has broken down the dividing wall
of hostility between us.

Ephesians 2:14

The Wall Came Tumbling Down (New York: Arch Cape Press, 1990), 58. Used by permission of AP/Wide World Photos.

During World War II, many Japanese Americans were placed in internment camps in the United States. Estelle Ishigo shows that a barbed wire fence does not stop children who want to fly a kite.

Estelle Ishigo, *Boys with Kite*, Special Collections, University Research Library, UCLA, Los Angeles, Calif. Used by permission.

5,000 Fed

Alemayehu Bizuneh, *Scene X of the Misereor "Hunger Cloth" from Ethiopia,* Aachen, Germany. Used by permission of Misereor Medienproduktion und Vertriebsbesellschaft mbH.

One of Jesus' disciples, Andrew, Simon Peter's brother, said to him, "There is a boy here who has five barley loaves and two fish. But what are they among so many people?" Then Jesus took the loaves, and when he had given thanks, he distributed them to those who were seated; so also the fish, as much as they wanted."

John 6:8–9, 11

This small boy helped Jesus to feed five thousand people. Jesus worked a miracle with the boy's gift of loaves and fishes. What gifts do you have to offer Jesus? What miracles might he work through you?

The report
on the miracle
of the bread and the fish
is about what happened
to somebody
who gave all he had.
It is, of course, a story about Jesus
multiplying all that bread and that fish.
But
whose bread did he multiply?
Whose fish did he divide?
  It all started
  with the real hero
  of that story:
  one small boy.

Joseph G. Donders, excerpt from"One Small Boy," in *The Jesus Community: Reflections on the Gospel for the B-Cycle* (Maryknoll, N.Y.: Orbis Books, 1981), 205. Used by permission of Joseph G. Donders.

One small boy gives all he has, and Jesus the Messiah feeds five thousand people.

The decision to feed the world is **the real decision.**

As the GRAINS of WHEAT

Words and music: Marty Haugen, 1991

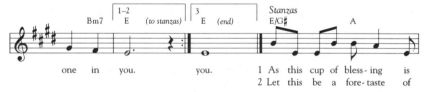

... I think that Jesus

praised that small boy

who had given all he had. . . .

When you are asked for something

you think you are unable to give,

think of that small boy

of this story,

and think of the twelve baskets

full of food given to him

because he gave

all he had.

You can help to feed others by offering your own "loaves and fishes." Think of seven items that you buy during the course of a month (for example, a soda, a movie, or a CD). If you are willing to give up these items this month and donate the money you would have spent on them to a program feeding hungry people, write them down on the loaves and fishes in the picture. Collect the money you have redirected and bring it to your *The Inviting Word* group four weeks from today.

Growing in Christ

But speaking the truth
in love, we must grow up
in every way into the
one who is the head,
into Christ.

Ephesians 4:15

Jyoti Sahi, *Jesus Christ—The Life of the World*, Nürnberg, Germany. Used by permission of Missionsprokur, der Oberdeutschen Jesuitenprovinz Sekretariat für Internationale Solidarität.

The name of this painting is *Jesus Christ—The Life of the World*. What in this painting makes you think about life? In what ways, if any, do the different parts of this painting remind you of your own daily life?

Teilhard de Chardin, priest, scientist, and teacher, says in *The Divine Milieu*: "God . . . is not far away from us, altogether apart from the world we see, touch, hear, smell and taste about us. Rather [God] awaits us every instant in our action, in the work of the moment. There is a sense in which [God] is at the tip of my pen, my spade, my brush, my needle—of my heart and of my thought."

Teilhard de Chardin, *The Divine Milieu* (New York: Harper Colophon Books, 1960), 64. © 1957 by Editions du Seuill, Paris. English translation © 1960 by Wm. Collins Sons & Co., London, and Harper & Row Publishers, Inc., N.Y. Renewed 1988 by Harper & Row. Used by permission of HarperCollins Publishers, Inc.

What are your gifts?

We Are Your People

We are your people:
Spirit of grace
you dare to make us
Christ to our neighbors
of every culture and place.

Joined in community,
treasured and fed,
may we discover
gifts in each other
willing to lead and be led.

Rich in diversity,
help us to live
closer than neighbors,
open to strangers,
able to clash and forgive.

Glad of tradition,
help us to see
in all life's changing,
where Christ is leading
where our best efforts should be.

Give, as we venture
justice and care
(peaceful, insisting,
risking, resisting),
wisdom to know when and where.

Spirit, unite us,
make us, by grace,
willing and ready,
Christ's living body,
loving the whole human race.

Write at least three of your special gifts—
skills, talents, special abilities—on this gift.

Touch of an Angel

Then Elijah lay down under the broom tree and fell asleep. Suddenly an angel touched him and said to him, "Get up and eat." He looked, and there at his head was a cake baked on hot stones, and a jar of water.

1 Kings 19:5–6a

Dieric Bouts, *Elijah and the Angel,* Altar of the Last Supper, Collegiale, St. Pierre, Louvain, Belgium (Erich Lessing/ Art Resource, N.Y.). Used by permission.

Even Elijah, God's faithful prophet, needed to be strengthened during a time of despair. God offered Elijah strength, nourishment, and hope.

Václav Havel, president of the Czech Republic, speaks eloquently about hope. Before he became president, he was sentenced to four-and-a-half years in prison for his involvement in the Czech human rights movement.

"The kind of hope I often think about (especially in situations that are particularly hopeless, such as prison) I understand above all as a state of mind, not a state of the world. Either we have hope within us or we don't; it is a dimension of the soul, and it's not essentially dependent on some particular observation of the world or estimate of the situation. . . . It is an orientation of the spirit, an orientation of the heart; it transcends the world that is immediately experienced, and is anchored somewhere beyond its horizons."

Václav Havel, *Disturbing the Peace: A Conversation with Karel Hvížďala* (New York: Alfred A. Knopf, 1990), 181.

"Do not depend on the hope of results. When you are doing the sort of work you have taken on, essentially an apostolic work, you may have to face the fact that your work will be apparently worthless and achieve no result at all, if not results opposite to what you expect. As you get used to this idea, you start more and more to concentrate not on the results but on the value, the truth of the work itself. And there, too, a great deal has to be gone through, as gradually you struggle less and less for an idea and more and more for specific people. The range tends to narrow down, but it gets much more real. In the end, it is the reality of personal relationships that saves everything."

Thomas Merton, letter to James Forest dated 21 February 1966, in *The Hidden Ground of Love: The Letters of Thomas Merton on Religious Experience and Social Concern*, selected and edited by William H. Shannon (New York: Farrar, Straus, Giroux, 1985), 294. Copyright © 1985 by the Merton Legacy Trust. Reprinted by permission of Farrar, Straus & Giroux, Inc.

"You can't die well if you're afraid, can you? We've known so many deaths, so many terrible deaths. Do you suppose I'll ever stop being afraid? Each candle I light, each candle that gutters down and dies brings me that much closer to my own death."

"No, Miss Livia," Honoria said. "That ain't so. You bin baptized, is you not? . . . We does our dying when we baptized, Miss Olivia. If it ain't done then, ain't never going to be done properly. When you is baptized your angel gives you a shove and you touch eternity, and eternity ain't got nothing to do with time at all. Once you brush against eternity, Miss Livvy, then time and death don't make no never-mind."

Madeleine L'Engle, *The Other Side of the Sun* (New York: Ballantine Books, 1971), 210–11. Copyright © 1971 by Madeleine L'Engle Franklin. Reprinted by permission of Farrar, Straus & Giroux, Inc.

Nothing can **trouble**, nothing can frighten. Those who seek God shall **never** go wanting. God alone fills us.

Seeking God's Purpose

Solomon prayed, "Give your servant therefore an understanding mind to govern your people, able to discern between good and evil; for who can govern this your great people?"

1 Kings 3:9

Marc Chagall, *Solomon*, as reproduced in *Bilder zur Bible* (Kunst-Buch-Galerie, Traudisch-Schröter, Wiehl, 1992), 61. © ARS. Used by permission.

My Definition of Purpose

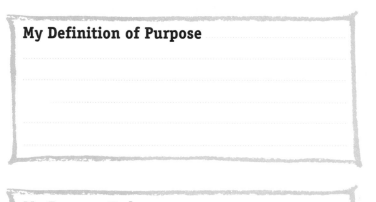

My Purpose Today

My Purpose This Year

Some of the images in Chagall's painting are drawn from his life. His native village burned when he was born. The image of burning houses often appears in his paintings and often represents suffering. The candelabra or menorah is a symbol of God's light and is the national symbol of the state of Israel. The beast suggests the sacrifice offered by Solomon. The arc above Solomon suggests a rainbow, which is a symbol of hope.

Chagall's symbols broaden the context of the world in which Solomon prays. God's good purposes are at work in Solomon's reign and in our world through experiences of suffering and of hope.

[Vocation] comes from the Latin *vocare,* to call, and means the work one is called to by God.

There are all different kinds of voices calling you to do all different kinds of work, and the problem is to find out which is the voice of God rather than of Society, say, or the Superego, or Self-interest.

By and large a good rule for finding out is this. The kind of work God usually calls you to do is the kind of work (a) that you need most to do and (b) that the world most needs to have done. If you really get a kick out of your work, you've presumably met requirement (a), but if your work is writing deodorant commercials, the chances are you've missed requirement (b). On the other hand, if your work is being a doctor in a leper colony, you have probably met requirement (b), but if most of the time you are bored and depressed by it, the chances are you have not only bypassed (a) but probably aren't helping your patients much either.

Neither the hair shirt nor the soft berth will do. The place God calls you to is the place where your deep gladness and the world's deep hunger meet.

Frederick Buechner, *Wishful Thinking: A Theological ABC* (New York: Harper & Row, 1973), 95. Copyright © 1973 by Frederick Buechner. Used by permission of HarperCollins Publishers, Inc.

But yield who will to their separation,
My object in living is to unite
My avocation and my vocation
As my two eyes make one in sight.
Only where love and need are one,
And the work is play for mortal stakes,
Is the deed ever really done
For heaven and the future's sakes.

Robert Frost, from "Two Tramps in Mud Time," in *The Complete Poems of Robert Frost* (New York: Holt, Rinehart and Winston, 1964). © 1936 Robert Frost. © renewed 1964 by Lesley Frost Ballantine. Used by permission.

About what do you think Taurian Osborne is praying? How might his Bible help him to discern God's purpose?

Jeffrey Allan Salter, *Taurian Osborne Prays at the New Fellowship Missionary Baptist Church,* Opa Laka, Florida. Used by permission.

The place God calls you to is the place where your deep gladness and the world's deep hunger meet.

Frederick Buechner, *Wishful Thinking: A Theological ABC* (New York: Harper & Row, 1973), 95. Copyright © 1973 by Frederick Buechner. Used by permission of HarperCollins Publishers, Inc.

The Dwelling Place

Then Solomon stood before the altar of God in the presence of all the assembly of Israel, and spread out his hands to heaven: "Hear the plea of your servant and of your people Israel when they pray toward this place; O hear in heaven your dwelling place; heed and forgive."

1 Kings 8:22, 30

Henri Matisse, *Chapel of the Rosary at Vence, France.* Photo by Hélène Adant.
Used by permission of Soeur Jacques Marie, Chapelle de Vence.

Where is God? Is God inside? Within a church sanctuary? At the communion table? At the pulpit? Sitting in the pews? Is God outside? In the trees and flowers? In the sky? The stars? In the vast oceans? On the mountaintops? In the desert?

Sacred Space

A sacred space is one in which a person feels the closeness of God. Such a space may be in a church, in a home, or in the natural world. Sometimes a sacred space contains special objects that help one to sense God's presence. A sacred space helps one enjoy a deeper experience of God, who dwells in and through all creation.

117

Monastery on Skellig Michael, Bord Failte Photo, Irish Tourist Board. Reproduction rights reserved. Used by permission.

God moves through the mystery of ancient stones and shrouds of white fog.

A Litany Based on **Psalm 84:1–5**

Group 1: How lovely is your dwelling place,

O God of hosts!

Group 2: My soul longs, even faints

for the courts of God;

my heart and flesh sing for joy

to the living God.

Group 1: Even the sparrow finds a home,

and the swallow a nest for herself,

where she may lay her young,

at your altars, O God of hosts,

my Ruler and my God.

Group 2: Blessed are those who dwell in your house,

ever singing your praise!

All: Blessed are those whose strength is in you,

in whose heart are the highways to Zion.

Inclusive-Language Psalms: Readings for Years A, B, and C (New York: The Pilgrim Press, 1987), 76. Used by permission.

Doers of the Word

But be doers of the word,
and not merely hearers who
deceive themselves.

James 1:22

Terri Franklin, *Volunteers Raising Roof Trusses*, detail, in "Building Houses Made of Straw," *Habitat World* (Habitat for Humanity), 12:3 (June 1995), 13. Used by permission.

Doers of the Word

**Read these words of Christian activists. What is your job as a "doer of the Word"?
What little things can you do well? What seeds can you sow?**

Our job . . . is to spread the Kingdom of Heaven, the Rule of God. Our business is to stop war,
to purify the world, to get it saved from poverty and riches, to make people like each other,
to heal the sick, and comfort the sad, to wake up those who have not yet found God,
to create joy and beauty wherever we go, to find God in everything and in everyone.

Muriel Lester, in *Ambassador of Reconciliation: A Muriel Lester Reader*, ed. Richard Deats
(Philadelphia: New Society Publishers, 1991), 93. Used by permission.

We need to be content with doing the little things and doing them well. And the little things
abound. The trouble is we're looking at the big things and we miss the beauty that's around,
the fact that people need affirmation is clear, people threatened with removal, groups struggling
for peace and justice, individual leaders to whom a word of encouragement might and will
make them go that extra mile in time of despair.

Rommel Roberts, as quoted by Vinton Deming, "An Interview with Rommel Roberts:
Nourishing the Small Seeds of Social Change," *Friends Journal*, January 1988. Used by permission.

We don't look for results, we are simply trying to be a ferment among the problems of the city;
we are on a pilgrimage of trust wherever we are in the world, simply trying to create links.
We sow and let others harvest.

From an interview with Brother Pedro, Taizé. Used by permission of Ateliers et Presses de Taizé.

Terri Franklin, *Volunteers Raising Roof Trusses*, in "Building Houses Made of Straw," *Habitat World* (Habitat for Humanity), 12:3 (June 1995), 13. Used by permission.

Habitat for Humanity builds sturdy, affordable houses in partnership with people who need them. These people are working on a Habitat for Humanity project, as do Christians from churches all over the world. This is one way to be a "doer of the Word."

Called as Partners in Christ's Service

Called as partners in Christ's service,
called to ministries of grace.
We respond with deep commitment,
fresh new lines of faith to trace.
May we learn the art of sharing,
side by side and friend with friend.
Equal partners in our caring
to fulfill God's chosen end.

Christ's example, Christ's inspiring,
Christ's clear call to work and worth.
Let us follow, never faltering,
reconciling folk on earth.
Men and women, richer, poorer,
all God's people, young and old.
Blending human skills together
gracious gifts from God unfold.

Thus new patterns for Christ's mission,
in a small or global sense,
Help us bear each other's burdens,
breaking down each wall or fence.
Words of comfort, words of vision,
words of challenge, said with care,
Bring new power and strength for action,
make us colleagues, free and fair.

So God grant us for tomorrow
ways to order human life
That surround each person's sorrow
with a calm that conquers strife.
Make us partners in our living,
our compassion to increase,
Messengers of faith, thus giving
hope and confidence and peace.

Partners in Christ's Service